THE COMPLETE SPROUTING COOKBOOK

Karen Cross Whyte

ILLUSTRATED BY RICHARD STORTROEN

TROUBADOR PRESS • SAN FRANCISCO

For Malcolm

Published in San Francisco by Troubador Press.

Printed in the United States of America.

Library of Congress Catalog Card Number: 72-92942
ISBN: 0-912300-25-6 (Softbound)
ISBN: 0-912300-28-0 (Hardbound)

TROUBADOR PRESS
126 Folsom Street
San Francisco, California 94105

CONTENTS

INTRODUCTION

The custom of sprouting seeds is more than twice as old as the Great Wall of China. In 2939 B.C., the Emperor of China recorded the use of "health giving sprouts" in a book about plants. Today, many people are familiar with sprouts only in Chinese cuisine, and usually only bean sprouts! Sprouting possibilities are expanding from beans to a wide variety of seeds. Alfalfa, wheat, corn and lentils are only a few of the seeds which are easily sprouted, economical, nutritious and tasty.

Scientists have found that as the seed germinates, many changes occur inside that increase the nutritional quality of the seed. Sprouts are high in protein, vitamins and minerals. They are considered a quick energy food, yet they are low in calories. Germinated seeds are organically pure since they need not be sprayed, dusted, dipped or chemically fertilized in any way.

Dry seed requires little storage room. Sealed in a jar and kept in a cool pantry, they will remain alive for up to 60 years or more. Lotus seeds, found at a dry lake bed in Manchuria, were germinated. These seeds were estimated to be 800 to 1200 years old! But for sprouting purposes, you will get maximum germination from seeds of the current year's crop.

The ancient practice of sprouting seeds is ideal for emergency food stockpiles, back-packing, space travel and expeditions of all kinds. In any season of the year, seeds can be converted into fresh succulent vegetables in two to six days. Seeds may be sprouted as food is required.

Economy is another excellent reason for raising sprouts. Food budgets are stretched tremendously by sprouting seeds. For example, a pound of alfalfa seed sprouts will fill a 10 gallon container. This is a bargain at only $1.30! Hospitals and large institutions faced with feeding many people can cut costs and raise their nutritional standards by growing and serving sprouts. Sprouting is an excellent way to beat the high cost of meat.

It is possible to have a sprout garden in your kitchen with very little time, space or equipment. The beginner needs only a wide-mouthed jar, a bit of cheesecloth and a rubber band. To untreated raw seeds, add moisture and a miniature hothouse is created in which many varieties of seeds will germinate. With this simple equipment, if need be, a kitchen farmer can grow enough sprouts to fill the family's entire requirement for fresh vegetables. This kind of weedless gardening does not require hard work, long hours, rich soil or favorable climatic conditions. And moreover, sprouts are naturally free of insects.

Many sprouts will keep crisp a week or more when properly stored in the refrigerator. Like any vegetable, the fresher they are the more flavor and food value they contain. Sprouts may be eaten raw, steamed, roasted or fried, but they are at their nutritional best when eaten raw. From appetizers to desserts, fresher vegetables cannot be found for use in every course of a meal. It is a happy and rewarding experience serving your home-grown sprouts, knowing that you are offering a new adventure in eating and a nutritionally superior food.

SEEDS AND CIVILIZATIONS

The evolution from hunting and food gathering to primitive farming is believed to have first occurred between 10 and 5 millennia B.C. One of the first areas to be settled is called the "Fertile Crescent." This fertile area is in the Near East, arching from the Mediterranean coast in the west around the Syrian Desert to Iraq in the east. Remains of wheat, peas and lentils have been found at Jarmo in Turkestan with a carbon date of about 5500 B.C.

Egyptian and Mesopotamian civilizations developed because of a favorable climate for cereal grains. Women may have been the first agriculturists, scattering seeds on patches of land while the men were occupied with hunting expeditions. The cultivation of grains supplied mankind with storable food. This year-round supply of food made it possible for communities to develop. Animal husbandry evolved along with a farming economy. Farming brought about other cultural developments as well. Planting and harvesting food crops led people to observe the movements of the heavenly bodies. This was the beginning of astronomy. Bartering of surplus food stocks between communities stimulated growth of language and the development of primitive writing for communication and record keeping. It has been said, with justification, that seeds of wheat were "the seeds of civilization."

The civilizations in ancient America were a product of those Indian tribes who knew best how to grow corn. Corn was so important to their culture that the plant was regarded as a supreme deity. This corn god was believed to have the power to bestow or withhold the harvest, reward man with an abundance of food, or punish him with famine.

The greater part of the diet of all the people in the world consists of seeds. Seventy percent of the world's protein consumption comes from grain crops. Rice is the main crop of Southern Asia. Sorghume and millet are staples in parts of China and Africa. Corn is popular in South Africa and Latin America. Barley, rye and oats also heavily contribute to the world's food supply.

Legume seeds, such as lentils, beans and peas, are the second largest group of seeds we use for food. These seeds have a huge protein content of 20 to 40 percent, and have been called the "poor man's meat." Legumes are also rich in carbohydrates. Some historians attribute the existence and survival of China to her use of soybeans as a food.

Nuts are also a rich source of seed food for man. The kernels of Brazil nuts, cashews, filberts, hazelnuts, pecans, walnuts and pine nuts are predominantly oily. Almonds and pistachio nuts are high in protein, while chestnuts are starchy.

Plant geneticists are working constantly to improve plant growth and seed quality. They have developed new strains of wheat which are not only higher in protein, but are more resistant to drought and insects. For years the inadequacy of corn as a protein source has caused severe malnutrition among children where corn is the principal food. Corn is dangerously lacking in lysine, the essential amino acid. Fifty percent of corn's protein is zein, which is indigestible to humans. Recently a new type of high protein corn has been developed with lower zein and increased lysine. Such plant improvements will enrich diets the world over.

According to many forecasts, the importance of seeds will continue to grow. The need to grow crops on land now used to maintain animals will lead to a decline in meat consumption in industrial countries. Even the eventual disappearance of meat is predicted by some experts. In many areas where meat is scarce, protein seed crops are particularly important.

An acre of land will yield more edible plant food if the seed harvest is sprouted. For example, an acre can produce as much as 385 pounds of alfalfa seed from a pound planted. If 384 pounds were sprouted for food, the yield would be approximately 3180 pounds of sprouts.

In the future we will have to make the best use of all food crops, wasting nothing in order to meet the demands of increasing population and shrinking farmlands. Sprouting is an excellent way to develop the full potential of seed crops.

NUTRITION

Grains, seeds and nuts have played a major role in the diet of man due to the high percentage of protein found in these foods. They contain from 7 to 40 percent protein. Since grains and seeds often are used as a source of protein in the diet, it is important to know how protein is related to maintaining a healthy body.

Protein comes from the Greek word *protos,* meaning "first". Nutritionists call protein "the building blocks" of good health. Every part of the body relies on protein for proper growth and repair. The body is largely made up of protein; your skin, muscles, internal organs, nails, hair, brain and even your bones contain protein. It is the basic element in protoplasm, which is the living, jelly-like substance of every cell. Food protein provides nitrogen and amino acids for the synthesis of body protein and other nitrogen-containing substances.

Thirty-two amino acids have been discovered, but only twenty-two of them are understood. If we get eight of these amino acids in our food we can manufacture the others required. These special eight amino acids cannot be synthesized and are thus called "essential." They must be provided in adequate amounts by dietary protein. The eight essential amino acids are isoleucine, leucine, lysine, methionine, phenylalanine, threonine, tryptophan and valine. Excess protein serves only as a source of energy.

Most legumes, grains and nuts contain the essential amino acids. Some, however, are low in one or more essential amino acids. In order to make full use of any food protein the amino acids must be properly balanced. Such balanced proteins are called "complete." Proteins that contain insufficient amounts of any of the essential amino acids are called "incomplete" or "limited." When two or more kinds of seeds containing "limited" protein are eaten at the same meal, one may supply the amino acid lacking in the other; together they become a "complete" protein. For example, corn has a small amount of lysine and a large amount of methionine, while beans are rich in lysine and somewhat deficient in methionine. Corn tortillas and beans served together provide a balanced combination of essential amino acids.

Dr. W. R. Aykrod, a nutritional director, states that "in the raw state, many legumes contain substances which are indigestible or even antagonistic to digestion such as saponins, glycosides, alkaloids, conjugates of protein with phytin or hemicellulose, and substances which inhibit the action of the digestive enzyme, trypsin." Mature raw legumes or legumes not properly prepared for consumption may in fact be poisonous and contain a good deal of indigestible material. Adequate soaking, sprouting, prolonged cooking, mashing and a variety of fermentation procedures have been used since ancient times to remove toxins from legumes and enhance their digestibility. Germination is one of the best methods of preparation and allows the whole seed to be eaten in a palatable form. Legumes also lose their objectionable gas generating quality when sprouted.

It is generally agreed by nutritionists that foods high in water content are more easily broken down and assimilated by the body. Seeds are concentrated foods in the sense that they have low water content. Most seeds are about 12 percent water; when sprouted the water content may increase to as much as 95 percent.

The process of sprouting seeds creates a more usable form of protein in many seeds. Sprouting also stimulates other beneficial changes. One impressive change is the increasing of vitamin C which takes place during sprouting of seeds. The vitamin C in oats increases 600 percent after sprouting! The knowledge that sprouts could cure and prevent scurvy was available in 1782, long before ascorbic acid was discovered and labeled vitamin C in 1920.

Dr. Paul Burkholder of Yale University tested the nutritional contents of oat sprouts. He found that the sprouted oats contained 500 percent more nicotinic acid, biotin had increased 50 percent, pantothenic acid 200 percent, pyridonine (B6) 500 percent, folic acid 600 percent, inositol 100 percent, thiamine (B1) 10 percent, and vitamin B2, 1350 percent.

Other studies of seeds and grains have yielded equally dramatic results. Dr. Chattepadhyay and his associates in Calcutta tested mung beans, lentils, peas, corn, rice and wheat for their vitamin E content. As a result of sprouting, the vitamin E content had increased up to 33 percent during a period of from two to four days. Vitamin A had increased in some seeds after sprouting for four days.

Even though complete research on the nutritional content of all sprouted seeds has not been made, there is more than enough scientific evidence available to conclude that sprouting a seed enhances its already high nutritional value.

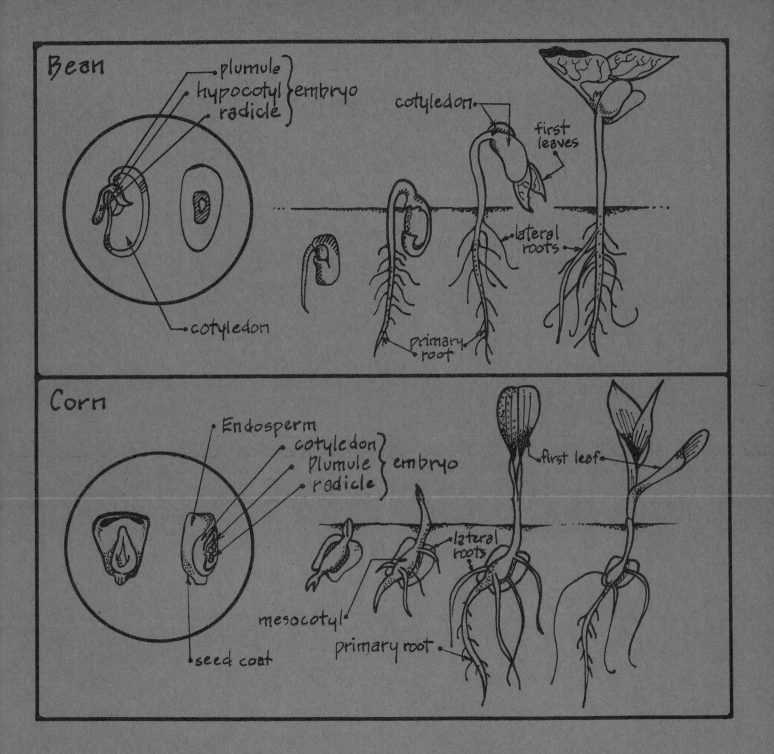

FROM SEEDS TO SPROUTS

A seed is a miniature plant in an arrested state of development. Its primary function is to propagate its species. Carbohydrates, proteins and fats are stored within the seed as a source of available nutrition when growth resumes. This storehouse of food is also nutritious for man. During the germination process, stored food is changed into a more usable form for both the plant and man.

The dry seed, when its activities are at a minimum, is in a dormant condition. Its food is held in reserve until the time and place are suitable for the start of new growth. Each species has its own built-in protection against heat, cold, drought and water. When the temperature, oxygen, light and moisture requirements are met, the seed will germinate. Sometimes a seed will wait several years for the right climactic combination before starting growth.

The outward appearance of seeds varies greatly in color, size, shape and form. Most plants can be identified by their seeds alone. The basic structure of all seeds is similar. Food reserve supplies are accumulated in the *endosperm,* (nourishment which surrounds the embryo) of corn and grains. These plants are called *monocots* (plants with single seed leaves). In *dicots* (plants with two seed leaves) such as beans and peas, the endosperm is absorbed by the *cotyledons* (seed leaves). The cotyledons serve as the food storage organ. The chief activity of the cotyledon and endosperm is the digestion and translocation of its reserve food to the embryo, which is the rudimentary growing part of the seed. Translocation is a process by which the sugars and amino acids move to the embryo for utilization in its growth and development.

The first step toward germination is the absorbing of water by the seed. This process is called imbibition. The seed coat is softened by the water, allowing the embryo and endosperm or cotyledon to "plump" itself with moisture. As the seed continues to swell, the seed coat is ruptured, freeing the embryo for continued development.

Dry seeds contain approximately 5 to 12 percent water. This proportion is increased up to 70 percent after a preliminary soaking of 12 hours. The amount of moisture around a seed affects the amount of oxygen available to it.

Respiration in dry seeds is extremely slow. Respiration is the metabolic process by which a plant or animal oxidizes its food materials. This process provides the living system with the energy it requires for the synthesis of new raw material and growth. After a definite amount of water is absorbed, a marked increase in seed respiration occurs. Even before we can see any growth, this increase of respiration is releasing energy for sprouting. As growth proceeds, the increasing demand for energy materials and new tissue is met by the digestion of reserve food. Starch is digested into sugar, lipids (oils) are changed to soluble compounds and storage proteins become amino acids.

The first visible evidence of germination is the breaking of the root tip through the seed covering. The growth of the primary root prior to the growth of the stem and leaves is nature's way of anchoring the seed and providing for further water absorption. Stem and leaf development follow. The seed becomes a little plant independent enough to absorb outside nourishment.

The temperature range for germinating seeds is generally between 32° and 113° F. A low percentage of germination may be expected at either extreme. For most crop plants, the optimum temperature lies between

68° and 86° F.; however, peas, lettuce, radishes, rye, barley and wheat will germinate readily at temperatures as low as 50° F.

Light does not influence the germination of most kinds of seeds, but germination of some is controlled by the presence or absence of light. Light also affects the flavor and the amount of chlorophyll contained in sprouts. Alfalfa, cress and other types of leafy sprouts should be "greened" in light for more chlorophyll and better flavor. Beans and sunflower seeds are more tasty if grown in the dark. In some seeds, exposure to light during the sprouting process inhibits the development of vitamin C.

Some sprouts should be harvested before the first leaves are fully developed. Sunflower seeds, for example, are tastiest when the root is only as long as the seed. Wheat and other grains are also best when the leaves are underdeveloped and the root is short. Alfalfa sprouts, however, should be between 2 and 2½ inches with 2 green leaves. Fenugreek may have roots as long as 3 inches. To prevent further growth, store sprouts in the refrigerator when they reach the desired length.

HOW TO BUY AND STORE SEEDS

When buying seeds for sprouting, select only those sold for growing purposes. The Department of Agriculture has strict regulations governing the viability or germination percentage of seeds sold as "seed-quality." These seeds are alive and a high percentage of germination may be expected. Legumes and grains sold in food markets, unless otherwise labeled, are "food-quality" seeds. There are no regulations of viability of these seeds; many may be dead and therefore will not sprout.

Only untreated seeds should be used for sprouting. Many "seed-quality" seeds have been treated to prevent or reduce losses from diseases caused by organisms associated with the seed or present in the soil. Some are treated with insecticide-fungicide mixtures and others with mercury compounds. Seeds treated with such chemicals can be poisonous if consumed.

Most health food stores stock viable grains, nuts and legumes suitable for sprouting. Many brands of pre-packed vegetable seeds sold in nurseries or garden shops have been treated. (W. Atlee Burpee Co. pre-packs seeds which are not treated.) Untreated garden and herb seeds can be obtained in bulk from seed companies such as Ferry-Morse Seed Co. and W. Atlee Burpee Co. Be sure to specify "untreated seeds" when ordering by mail.

It is important to select seeds of good quality. Before purchasing seeds, check for discoloration, cracks, breaks and other imperfections. Sunflower seeds turn yellowish when they become old, and those packed in plastic bags may have many broken kernels. Dead or damaged seeds will not sprout, but can ferment, causing decay of the remaining good seeds during germination.

To keep seeds in a viable condition, they must be stored properly, especially if large quantities are stored for a long period. *Seeds should be stored dry and kept dry.* Only sealed metal, plastic or glass containers will keep seeds dry. Coffee tins, plastic freezer containers or glass jars with tightly fitting plastic or metal lids are good moisture-proof containers. Canning labels can be used to identify seeds stored in cans or used on transparent containers until you are able to identify your seeds by sight. Dating the label will help keep track of storage time. Put your containers of seeds in a cool, dry and dark place. Most seeds will remain in good condition for 3 or 4 months if stored at room temperature in a pantry or cupboard. Commercially stored seeds are sometimes kept at temperatures near freezing or below. If you buy seeds in bulk, they can be stored for longer periods in a refrigerator. Be certain, however, that the refrigerated container is impervious to moisture.

METHODS OF SPROUTING

First read the directions for the individual seed for special instructions and the selection of the proper method of sprouting.

Measure seeds and pick them over carefully, retaining only good whole seeds for sprouting. Broken seeds tend to ferment. Wash seeds well and place in a bowl or jar with lukewarm water. Use four cups of water to one cup of seeds. Soak overnight. Drain, retaining soaking liquids to be used as stock in soups or beverages. Do not soak seeds which are to be sprouted by the sprinkle method.

According to Lelord Kordel, a leading nutritionist, the mineral content of sprouts can be increased by adding one to two teaspoonsful of dried kelp to each quart of water used for soaking. Kordel claims this will increase the available iodine and other minerals in sprouts.

Put seeds in sprouting container, if not there already, and rinse thoroughly. Drain off all excess water. Keep seeds in a warm area where temperature will remain even. Size of container will depend on amount of seeds to be sprouted. Container must be large enough for growth and air circulation.

During the winter, your house may become too cold at night to germinate certain seeds. This problem can be overcome by wrapping the sprouting container in a piece of flannel or a terrycloth towel and placing it near a light bulb. The lighted bulb will give added warmth. Leave the end open for air circulation. A suitable place to sprout seeds in the winter may be your oven, if the light is left on and the oven door is ajar. Be sure to check the oven temperature first to make certain it remains within the desired temperature range.

After the sprouts have grown to desired length, the chlorophyll content of the leaves can be increased by placing the sprouts in the light until leaves become green. This "greening" process takes only a few hours if the sprouts are placed in artificial light or in indirect sunlight.

Jar Method

Equipment:

Widemouth jar

Cheesecloth, nylon net, nylon stocking or plastic screen

Rubber band, jar ring or string

Place pre-soaked seeds in the jar (pre-soaking can be done directly in the jar). Cover opening with a piece of cheesecloth, nylon net or piece of nylon stocking; hold in place with a rubber band or string. A piece of plastic screen cut to fit inside a jar ring also works very well. Rinse and drain seeds two to four times a day depending on the type of seed and the weather. In warm, dry weather, the water evaporates quickly. Cover the jar with a brown paper bag if you plan to leave it out in the light. Lay the jar in a bowl, mouth down at a slight angle to catch further drainage. Keep the sprouting jar in a cupboard for darkness and a more even temperature. The cupboard door may be left ajar for air circulation. When sprouts are the desired length, remove the bag and place the jar in the light for "greening" of the sprouts.

Flower Pot Method

Equipment:

New unglazed clay flower pot with a clay dish

Plastic screen or nylon net

Wash flower pot thoroughly. Soak it in clear water for a few hours or overnight to prevent the porous clay from absorbing moisture from the seeds. Cut a piece of plastic screen or two layers of nylon net to fit the inside bottom of the pot. Place the net or screen in the bottom of the pot to prevent the seeds from falling through the drain hole. Put the pre-soaked seeds on top of the screen. To rinse, place the pot in the sink and pour lukewarm water over the seeds. Drain. Set the pot in the clay dish to catch any further draining. Damp paper towels or a damp piece of cardboard cut to fit the inside top makes a cover. The cover helps maintain a moist atmosphere, but it should fit loosely so air can circulate around the seeds. Rinse two to four times a day, depending on the type of seed and the weather. Rinse more often in warm, dry weather. If sprouts are to be "greened," put them in a clear glass bowl when they have reached the desired length. Cover the bowl with a clear piece of plastic. It should fit loosely for air circulation. Keep the sprouts in indirect sunlight or near artificial light until their leaves turn green. Refrigerate in a covered container.

It is very important to keep your sprouting equipment clean. If seeds should ferment in your clay pot, scrub it thoroughly with soap and water. The porous clay may contain bacteria that even a brush can't remove. Put the washed pot in a saucepan, cover with water and boil for ten minutes to sterilize it.

Paper Towel Method

Equipment:

Glass tray or stainless steel pan with draining rack

Paper towels

Place the rack inside the tray. The rack makes it possible for the air to circulate more freely around seeds. Soak a two-layer thickness of paper towels in water. Squeeze out excess water. Spread the damp towels over the rack, leaving room at two ends for air circulation. Scatter pre-soaked seeds evenly over the surface of the towels. Cover loosely with another double thickness of moist towels (do not cover with paper towels when sprouting oats). Slip container into a plastic bag, leaving the end open for air circulation. Place in the cupboard for darkness, leaving the door slightly ajar. To water the seeds, remove the top layer of towels. Sprinkle the seeds with water and re-soak the top layer of towels, squeezing out excess moisture each time. Water only enough to provide a moist atmosphere.

Sprinkle Method

Equipment:

Glass tray, Pyrex pie plates or stainless steel pans

Plastic wrap or aluminum foil

Do not pre-soak seeds for this method. This method is designed for seeds that become gelatinous when water is added to them. Gelatinous seeds do not drain well and may decay from too much moisture. Measure equal amounts of water and seed. Pour water into container and sprinkle the seeds evenly over the water. Let seeds stand for about one hour and check to see if they need more water or there is an excess. If they appear dry, sprinkle a little more water over them. Tip the container slightly and carefully pour off any water that flows to the side. The seeds will have formed a solid jelly-like mass and will remain in place if draining is done carefully.

Cover the container with a piece of loosely fitted foil or slip into a large plastic bag. If a bag is used, leave the end open for air circulation. Keep in the cupboard, or in the light if foil is used. Sprinkle a small amount of water over seeds as required. Once a day is enough, except in hot, dry weather. When the sprouts are the desired length, place them in indirect sunlight or artificial light for "greening."

HOW TO STORE SPROUTS

Before storing, let sprouts drain three or four hours after the last rinse. They will keep better if no excess moisture clings to the sprouts. Store sprouts loosely in sealed glass jars or covered plastic containers. Plastic bags are not recommended since the delicate sprouts tend to get crushed. Damaged sprouts are quick to decay. Most sprouts will keep crisp as long as a week, but for better flavor and nutrition sprout only what you can use in three or four days. Grain sprouts should be stored in the coldest part of the refrigerator (about 35°) as some types continue to grow even after refrigeration. Some sprouts can be frozen, but it is not recommended since the roots and leaves become limp upon defrosting. If you have an over-supply, share them with your neighbors or feed them to your pets. Birds and rodents eat sprouts. Dogs and cats will eat them when mixed with their regular food.

SEEDS FOR SPROUTING

On the following pages, in alphabetical order, is a list of seeds suitable for successful sprouting. You need not limit yourself to those listed: any edible seed which does not produce a noxious plant can be sprouted for food. Tomato and potato plants are poisonous and the seeds should not be used for sprouting.

Adzuki Beans

Adzuki beans have been cultivated for centuries in Japan, Korea, China and Manchuria. In Japan, when these small red beans are cooked, mashed and sweetened, they are used as a filling for cakes. The beans are pounded into a fine meal used for making cakes and confectionery which are often served as special festival dishes. Adzuki beans were an important ingredient in foods cooked in honor of the birthday of the Emperor of Japan.

The beans are 25 percent protein and a rich source of the essential amino acid, lysine. Except for tryptophan, they contain all the other essential amino acids. Adzuki beans have a high content of iron, niacin and calcium.

Sprouting method	jar or flower pot
Temperature	68° to 86°, best at 72°
Rinse	4 times a day
Harvest length	1 inch
Sprouting time	about 4 days
Yield	½ cup seeds makes about 2 cups sprouts

Alfalfa Seeds

Alfalfa is widely cultivated for forage. Domestic animals have long benefited from this highly nutritious plant. The word alfalfa comes from an Arabic phrase, *al-fachfacha* which means "very good fodder." A recent use of alfalfa is for a commercial source of chlorophyll.

Scientists have discovered that sprouted seeds are "good fodder" for man. The sprouts are a good source of such important vitamins as D, E, G, K and U. They contain the vital cell building amino acids, arginine, lysine, theronine and triptophane. Alfalfa sprouts are a rich source of minerals such as phosphorus, chlorine, iron, silicone, aluminum, calcium, magnesium, sulfur, sodium and potassium. Because of the especially high chlorophyll content of alfalfa, it contributes to the healing process and sweetens the breath. The seeds are about 35 percent protein, which is higher than most meats. It is easy to see why alfalfa has been called the "king of sprouts."

The flavor of alfalfa sprouts is one that everyone will enjoy. They are excellent in sandwiches, salads, soups and egg dishes. When harvested before green leaves appear and the root is only ⅛ inch long, they still contain a comparatively concentrated percentage of protein. They can then be ground and added to recipes for pastries, breads and cakes, creating a high protein food.

Sprouting method	jar or flower pot
Temperature	68° to 86°, best at 72°
Rinse	twice a day
Harvest length	1½ to 2 inches greened or ⅛ inch
Sprouting time	3 to 5 days (24 hours for ⅛ inch)
Yield	3 T seed makes 1 qt. greened sprouts
	¼ cup makes 1½ cups ⅛ inch sprouts

Almonds

Almonds are native to Persia, where they have been used as a remedy for insomnia and dysentery. They have also been used to increase the milk supply of nursing mothers, as well as help relieve headaches and hangovers. "To guard against intoxication and prevent hangovers, eat five almonds before drinking alcoholic beverages," is an old Persian adage. In ancient lore, almonds were believed to be an antidote to the influence of witchcraft and the evil eye.

Almonds are superior to other nuts in their protein content, which is about 18 percent. They are an alkaline food rich in calcium and potassium. When sprouted, they are crisp and crunchy. Almond sprouts are delicious eaten out of the hand as a snack or used in your favorite recipes in place of unsprouted almonds.

Sprouting method	paper towel
Temperature	68° to 86°
Rinse	2 to 3 times a day
Harvest length	when root is ⅛ to ¼ inch
Sprouting time	3 or 4 days
Yield	½ cup makes ¾ cup sprouts

Barley

The origin of barley is unknown, but it is known to have been cultivated since prehistoric times in many parts of the world. Barley was grown in Switzerland during the Stone Age. The ancient Greeks fed it to their training athletes in the form of barley-mush. In Chinese lore, barley was considered a symbol of male potency. The Hindus use barley grains in many religious celebrations, marriage, birth and death rites.

Barley has a lower protein content than wheat. It has less gluten than wheat and does not mix easily with water to form a paste or dough for bread. For this reason it has gradually been replaced by wheat in breadmaking. Presently its chief use is in malt production for the brewing industry and for animal foodstuffs.

Barley sprouts are delicious when added to soups, salads and breads. For a special treat, grind them in a nut mill and add to pancake batter.

Sprouting method	jar or flower pot
Temperature	70° to 80°
Rinse	2 or 3 times a day
Harvest length	when root is length of seed
Sprouting time	3 or 4 days
Yield	½ cup makes 1 cup sprouts

Beans

The following beans are discussed in this section: black beans, great northern white beans, fava, haricot, kidney, lima, navy, pinto, red and Windsor (broad beans). Adzuki, soy, garbanzo and mung beans are listed individually.

There are many varieties of beans, a number of which have been cultivated by man since the dawn of civilization. For centuries they have been common food in most countries.

Prehistoric man in North Africa cultivated broad beans. Broad bean deposits have been found in Switzerland dating back to the Bronze Age. The kidney bean is a native of the Americas and has been used by man for over 6000 years. Remains of these beans have been found in caves in Mexico and radiocarbon-dated at 4000 B.C. Kidney beans were also discovered in Pre-Inca Peruvian tombs.

Historically, in some parts of the world, beans have been shunned by certain classes of society and regarded as poor man's meal. The ancient Egyptians cultivated beans, but the priests and ruling class considered them unworthy food. Beans were left to the common people. The ancient Greeks and Romans cloaked beans with superstitions. Beans were considered to be unlucky and connected with death. The little black spot (hilm) on their skin was believed to be an omen of death. They were used as offerings of sacrifice to the god Apollo, but the priests of Jupiter were forbidden to touch or speak of them.

The "poor man's meat" concept of beans belongs essentially to Europe and the Near East, and does not apply to all countries. Beans were a major part of the diet of the original inhabitants of the

Americas and are still a staple food throughout much of Central and South America. The early colonists of North America enriched their meals with locally grown beans and learned to enjoy their flavor as much as corn.

Beans and other legumes are our richest source of protein in the vegetable kingdom. The protein content of beans ranges from 20 to 25 percent, except soybeans, which may contain as much as 40 percent. Beans are an excellent source of iron, niacin, phosphorus, potassium, vitamin B1 and B2. A good amount of calcium is present in beans.

Most beans are easily sprouted and can be used in many ways. All varieties are delicious when ground and cooked as patties or baked in vegetable loaves. Beans add crunchy texture to salads and soups. Each variety of bean sprouts has its own individual flavor.

Sprouting method	jar or flower pot
Temperature	68° to 86°
Rinse	3 or 4 times a day
Harvest length	1 to 2 inches
Sprouting time	3 to 5 days
Yield	1 cup seeds makes about 4 cups of sprouts

Buckwheat

Botanically, buckwheat is not considered a true cereal. Because its seeds yield a flour used in breads and breakfast foods, it is often referred to as a grain cereal. This annual plant gets its name from the German word *buchweizen,* "beechwheat." Buckwheat seeds are small and triangular, resembling the beech nut. Another name for buckwheat is Saracen wheat.

Buckwheat is native to Siberia and Manchuria; it has been grown extensively in China from prehistoric times. Buckwheat was imported by Japan and Russia and then introduced to Europe. It is a staple of Holland and is now cultivated in many other parts of the world. In the United States, cultivation of buckwheat has declined considerably since 1935 when it was a major crop. Today the seeds are used primarily for griddle-cake flour, groats, kasha and livestock food.

Because buckwheat is naturally blight resistant, it is seldom sprayed with insecticides, even when grown commercially. The plant matures quickly (about 10 weeks) and has a long blooming period. Its white flowers attract bees. Buckwheat honey is dark, flavorful and one of the most nutritious honeys produced in this country. The luxuriant foliage of buckwheat gives the crop the ability to smother weeds. When plowed under buckwheat decays quickly making an excellent green manure. It will thrive in poor, hilly, unimproved grounds, and has been grown as cover for a variety of game birds and other wild life.

Buckwheat is about 12 percent protein and contains a good supply of phosphorus, potassium, iron, niacin and calcium. Rutin, a flavonol gycoside used in the treatment of vascular disorders, is an extract of buckwheat. Rutin prevents vitamin C from being destroyed in the body by oxygen and is used in vitamin C tablets.

Two days is all that is required to produce delicious sprouts from buckwheat seeds. The sprouts are as versatile as the plant. They can be used in soups, salads, griddle-cakes, muffins, noodles and vegetable loaves. They are delicious just steamed and eaten with butter.

Be sure to buy raw seeds for sprouting. Most buckwheat groats are roasted and sold for making kasha. Rinse the seeds thoroughly but do not pre-soak. Enough moisture will be retained by the seeds to start germination. If pre-soaked, the water becomes slightly gelatinous and it is difficult to drain the seeds sufficiently.

Sprouting method	paper towel or jar
Temperature	68° to 80°
Sprinkle or rinse	once a day or as required
Harvest length	when root is ¼ to ½ inch long
Sprouting time	2 to 3 days
Yield	1 cup makes 3 cups sprouts

Chia Seeds

The Indians of California, Arizona, New Mexico, Nevada and Mexico used chia seeds on their hunting expeditions to help fortify the body against the exhaustive effects of the desert heat. It has been said that the Indians lived on chia seeds alone for many days.

The most important of the chia-yielding sage plants is known as *Salvia columbaria*. The seeds are remarkably rich in potassium, copper, calcium, phosphorus, iron, magnesium and iodine. Like flax, chia seeds are a good source of vegetable fat and protein.

Due to their protective coating, it is difficult for the body to assimilate any kind of seed in their whole form. Therefore, it is best to soak, grind or sprout chia seeds before using. If the sprouts are harvested when the root is about ⅛ inch long, they can be ground in a blender with a little water and added to breads and pancakes. When fully sprouted with two green leaves, they have a pungent flavor and add zest to soups, salads, dips, sandwiches and spreads.

Sprouting method	sprinkle
Temperature	68° to 86°
Sprinkle with water	once a day or as required
Harvest length	1 to 1½ inches greened or ⅛ inch ungreened
Sprouting time	about 4 days for green sprouts or 24 hours for ⅛ inch sprouts
Yield	2 T seed makes 3 to 4 cups 1½ inch sprouts. ¼ cup seed makes 1 cup ⅛ inch sprouts.

Chick-peas

Chick-peas are called *gram* in India, *garbanzo* in Spain, Mexico and the Philippines. These drought-resisting legumes originated in the Mediterranean region. They are now grown throughout the sub-tropics and in the cool season in the dry tropics, particularly in India.

Chick-pea sprouts are considered to be very nourishing and are delicious when added to soups, salads, curries or served slightly cooked as a vegetable. Chick-peas are 20 percent protein, a good source of iron, and have trace quantities of vitamin A and C. When sprouted, vitamin A and C are increased.

Sprouting method	flower pot or jar
Temperature	68° to 72°
Rinse	4 to 6 times per day
Harvest length	when root is ½ inch long
Sprouting time	about 3 days
Yield	1 cup seed makes 3 cups sprouts

Corn

Corn is essentially an American grain. Indians have cultivated corn for over 5000 years. There has been little basic botanical change in the plant. Changes in the size of the plant and in its productivity, however, have been tremendous. An entire ear of primitive corn produced less food than that contained in a single kernal of some modern varieties. These prehistoric ears were only ¾ to one inch long.

A Narraganset Indian legend tells how, in ancient times, a crow came to the hunting grounds. The crow brought a kernal of corn in one ear and a bean in the other. This is how the vegetable crops originated. In gratitude, the Indians allowed the crows to feast in their corn and bean fields unmolested. The birds were entitled to part of the harvest which one of their ancestors had made possible. Ripe and dried corn is ground, and the meal or flour is used to make many kinds of pastries, cakes, breads, snacks and cereals. Sprouted corn can be used in soups, stews, casseroles and, when ground, in breads. The sprouts have a delicious sweet flavor.

Sprouting method	flower pot or jar
Temperature	72° to 86°
Rinse	2 or 3 times a day
Harvest length	½ inch root
Sprouting time	2 to 3 days
Yield	1 cup corn makes 2 cups sprouts

Garden Cress

Garden cress is an annual plant often used in winter salads. Because of its rapid growth, it derives its name from the Latin word *crescere,* which means, "to grow." Its peppery flavor adds spice to vegetable salads, cole slaw and to sour cream and cucumbers. Do not cook this vegetable: it can be added to cooked foods after they have been removed from the heat. Dried, powdered seeds are sometimes used as a salt substitute.

Cress contains huge amounts of vitamin A and C. The plant contains 9300 IU of vitamin A and 69 milligrams of vitamin C per hundred grams of edible plant.

Sprouting method	jar or sprinkle
Temperature	50° to 68°
Rinse or sprinkle	twice a day
Harvest length	1½ inch greened
Sprouting time	3 or 4 days
Yield	1 T seed makes 1½ cups sprouts

Fenugreek

Fenugreek is a native legume of Western Asia, but gets its name from a Latin word which means "Greek hay." The plant is used in Oriental cooking and the seeds are used in candy to give it a maple flavor. In India the chief use of the seeds is for flavoring curries and making commercial curry powder.

Fenugreek contains the fat controlling factor, choline, which is increased in the sprouted seed. The seeds have long been believed to possess healing factors that aid in the treatment of gastric and other intestinal disorders, including ulcers. A tea made from the seed also has been used as a gargle for sore throat.

The seeds and plant are extremely rich in iron. The plant has an abundance of vitamin A. The seeds are 29 percent protein.

Fenugreek sprouts are mildly spicy to slightly bitter in flavor. Use fenugreek sprouts when you want to add piquancy to bland foods. The sprouts are excellent in salads, soups and curries.

Sprouting method	jar or flower pot
Temperature	68° to 86°
Rinse	1 or 2 times a day
Harvest length	3 inches, greened
Sprouting time	4 to 5 days
Yield	¼ cup seed makes about 4 cups sprouts

Flax Seeds

Flax seeds have long been used in folk medicine remedies of all kinds. Oil from flax seeds is thought to be good for coughs, asthma and pleurisy. Ground seeds mixed with boiling water have been used in poultices.

The seeds contain 23 percent protein and 5.5 milligrams of niacin per 100 grams of seed. They also have healthy quantities of calcium and iron.

The deep green sprouts have a mild flavor and are a good substitute for lettuce in sandwiches. They also add color and variety to salads and soups.

Sprouting method	jar or pot
Temperature	68° to 78°
Rinse	2 or 3 times a day
Harvest length	1 to 2 inches, greened
Sprouting time	about 4 days
Yield	2 T makes 1½-2 cups sprouts

Lentils

Lentils are native to central Asia where they have been cultivated since prehistoric times. Lentils are an annual herb with many varieties which are grown as a cold season crop throughout the subtropics, particularly in India, Africa and Central and South America. India is the leading producer and consumer.

The small brown or reddish varieties are generally considered to have a better flavor than the large yellow type. They are served at least once a day in most Indian homes. The protein content of lentils is 25 percent and they contain substantial amounts of vitamin B, iron and phosphorus. Lentils contain small amounts of vitamin C and E which are increased when sprouted. Lentil sprouts may be eater raw in salads or steamed lightly and served with butter or spices.

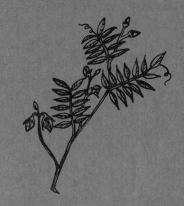

Sprouting method	flower pot or jar
Temperature	68° to 86°
Rinse	2 or 3 times a day
Harvest length	about 1 inch
Sprouting time	3 or 4 days
Yield	1 cup makes 6 cups sprouts

Millet

Millet is another cereal grass, like barley, cultivated by prehistoric man. It was known in ancient Babylon, Assyria and India. Today, a number of varieties of millet are produced in many countries. The pearly seeds of millet are the smallest of all cereal grains. In America they are cultivated mainly for use as cattle and poultry feed.

Whole millet is extremely rich in iron and niacin. It is also a source of protein, phosphrous and vitamin B2. This grain is the most alkaline of all cereals and the most easily digested. For this reason it is especially favored by older people. Millet has a delicious, sweet flavor similar to corn.

The flour of millet is white, and ideal for use in cakes and puddings. Sprouted millet, when mixed with wheat flour, makes excellent bread. The sprouts may be added to soups or steamed and served with butter and a little celery salt.

Sprouting method	jar or flower pot
Temperature	70° to 80°
Rinse	2 or 3 times a day
Harvest length	¼ inch root
Sprouting time	3 or 4 days
Yield	1 cup seed makes 2 cups sprouts

Mung Beans

Mung beans are extensively cultivated in India, Iran, Malaya, East Africa and Greece. They are also an important legume crop throughout a large part of the tropics. The beans are an annual herb with a short maturing period, often grown as a source of green manure. Mung beans are grown in the Orient for food as bean sprouts, a favorite ingredient in many Chinese and Philippine dishes. They are now very popular in the United States.

This legume is a good source of choline, which increases during sprouting. For example, mung beans contain 205 milligrams of choline per 100 grams before sprouting. After four days of sprouting, the amount of choline increased to 250 milligrams. The amount of vitamin E in four days of sprouting was increased from 2.4 milligrams to 3.4 milligrams.

Use mung beans in your favorite Oriental dishes, in soups, casseroles and salads or serve steamed with butter. Mung beans begin to loose their crispness after four days of storage.

Sprouting method	flower pot or jar
Temperature	68° to 86°
Rinse	3 or 4 times a day
Harvest length	about 2 inches
Sprouting time	3 or 4 days
Yield	1 cup seed makes 4 to 5 cups sprouts

Oats

Oats, along with its main consumer, the horse, are native to Tartary in central Asia. The cultivation of oats followed the horse to many countries. Although originally grown for animal food, oats have become a major crop in Norway, Sweden, Ireland, Scotland and the United States, where they are also used for human consumption. In the United States, oatmeal is a popular breakfast food and often used in cookies.

Oats are 14 percent protein and contain all the essential amino acids. They are rich in vitamin B1 and contain appreciable amounts of other B vitamins including riboflavin, niacin, choline, pantothenic acid and vitamin E. Oats have a good supply of minerals, such as phosphorus, iron, manganese, copper, fluorine and zinc.

Sprouted oats can be added to breads, cookies and soups or used for breakfast cereal, cooked or raw.

Oats require very little water for sprouting. They sour quickly when over-watered. Do not pre-soak oats, as they will absorb enough water from damp paper towels to stimulate germination. Wash grains quickly and drain *thoroughly* before spreading in a thin layer over the damp towels. To water, sprinkle the grains carefully or spray lightly with an atomizer.

Sprouting method	paper towel method
Temperature	70° to 80°
Rinse	once a day or only enough to keep the seeds moist
Harvest length	when lead root is length of seed (oats have 3 roots, 2 short and 1 long)
Sprouting time	3 or 4 days
Yield	1 cup seed makes 2 cups sprouts

Peas

Peas are an annual vine with many varieties, originating in the eastern Mediterranean. They are now grown in temperate regions throughout the world or as a cool season crop in the tropics. The seeds are eaten dried or immature. Until the 17th century, peas were eaten mainly in the dried form. Fresh green peas became popular after a craze for them flourished at the court of King Louis XIV. Madame de Maintenon described this passion for peas as "a fashion and a madness."

Dried peas are 22 percent protein and contain all eight of the essential amino acids. When sprouted they have a flavor similar to fresh peas.

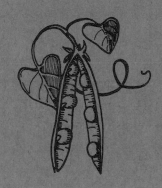

Sprouting method	flower pot or jar
Temperature	50° to 68°
Rinse	2 or 3 times a day
Harvest length	root is length of seed
Sprouting time	about 3 days
Yield	1½ cups seed makes 2 cups sprouts

Pumpkin Seeds

In China the pumpkin is the symbol of fruitfulness and health. It is called the Emperor of the Garden. The pumpkin is a member of the gourd family and native to India, but it is now naturalized and cultivated in almost every country throughout the world.

Pumpkin seeds have been used in folk medicine for centuries. The Hungarian gypsy, the Anatolian Turk and the mountain-dwelling Bulgarians all knew that pumpkin seeds preserved the prostate gland and thus, male potency. The seeds have also been used as a treatment against tapeworm, and to correct urinary disorders.

Pumpkin seeds have been found to be extremely high in phosphorus and iron. They contain 11.2 milligrams of iron per 100 grams of seed. Pumpkin seeds contain an abundance of B vitamins and small amounts of calcium and vitamin A. These wonderful seeds are 30 percent protein and rich in unsaturated fatty acids.

Use hulled seeds for sprouting. For best flavor, do not oversprout. Eat sprouted pumpkin seeds raw or lightly toasted. Put them in salads, soups, bread and candy.

Sprouting method	jar
Temperature	68° to 86°
Rinse	2 or 3 times a day
Harvest length	¼ inch root
Sprouting time	about 3 days
Yield	1 cup makes about 2 cups

Rice

Rice is a staple food for nearly half the world's population. It is not only one of the oldest, but also one of the most extensively cultivated of all grain cereals. According to Chinese legend, Emperor Sun-Nung (2800 - 2700 BC) taught his people the art of cultivating rice. Rice became a symbol of fertility. As such it was originally used by the Chinese and the Hindus to pelt newly wed couples in order to bring them good luck and many children.

There are reputedly 7000 different types of rice, each varying slightly. Generally, rice can be divided into three major types: long, medium and short grain. The long grain is four to five times as long as it is wide. When cooked, the grains will separate and the rice looks light and fluffy. The shorter, plumper grains of medium and short varieties cook tender and moist, but tend to cling together.

Whole brown rice is an excellent source of niacin and contains an appreciable amount of vitamin E. Rice has a small amount of vitamin C which is markedly increased when the grains are sprouted. The protein content of rice is only about seven percent, but it contains all eight of the essential amino acids.

Sprouting method	jar
Temperature	50° to 80°
Rinse	2 or 3 times a day
Harvest length	when root is length of seed
Sprouting time	3 or 4 days
Yield	1 cup seed makes 2½ cups sprouts

Rye

Rye is the hardiest of all cereal grasses and can be cultivated in soil too poor for any other grain crop. It is native to western Asia and the Near East. Because it furnishes an excellent malt, the largest part of the rye crop in Canada and the United States is used for distillation in the manufacture of liquors. In Europe the bulk of rye is ground into dark flour for a delicious black bread.

Rye will sprout easily in cool weather. It should be stored in the coldest part of the refrigerator after the desired length is obtained to retard further growth.

Rye is rich in manganese, phosphorus, potassium and iron. It contains 12 percent protein. Sprouted rye makes a good snack food eaten raw or it may be added to bread, soups and salads.

Sprouting method	jar
Temperature	50° to 68°
Rinse	2 or 3 times a day
Harvest length	when root is length of seed
Sprouting time	3 or 4 days
Yield	1 cup makes 3½ cups sprouts

Sesame

Sesame seeds are one of the first recorded seeds eaten by man. This herb is native to India, but is cultivated in many parts of the world, including the United States. Apart from being a popular ingredient in Asian cooking, sesame is used considerably in the Balkans and in Middle Eastern cooking. In the United States it is used in cakes, salads, candies and pastries.

Sesame is 50 percent fat and rich in the unsaturated fatty acids. Its oil can prevent rancidity in other oils and is often mixed with them for that purpose. When the seed is crushed for its oil the residual press-cake is used as a valuable source of protein.

Sesame seeds can be purchased in paste form, which can be converted into "milk" by adding water. This liquid stays fresh for a long time and is easily digested. Sesame milk has more calcium than cows' milk. One hundred grams of whole sesame seed contain 1125 milligrams of calcium, whereas two glasses of cows' milk contain only 500 milligrams.

Sesame seeds are 18 percent protein and a well-balanced source of essential amino acids. They are good suppliers of vitamin B1, niacin and small amounts of vitamin E. The abundance of calcium and lecithin makes sesame a valuable aid in preventing cholesterol from collecting in the blood.

Unhulled sesame seeds, which are required for sprouting, are difficult to find. Middle Eastern style delicatessens and health food stores may stock them. The already high nutritional content of the seeds is enhanced when they are sprouted. The sprouts can be used in many recipes in place of unsprouted seeds.

Sprouting method	jar
Temperature	68° to 80°
Rinse	4 or more times per day
Harvest length	when root is length of seed
Sprouting time	about 3 days
Yield	1 cup makes about 1½ cups sprouts

Soybeans

Soybeans have been part of Oriental cookery since 3000 B.C., but were not introduced in Europe until the end of the 17th century. Brought to America around 1804, soybeans did not become a major crop in the United States until 1924. Production increase since then has been phenomenal.

Hundreds of books have been published concerning various aspects of the soybean industry. Soybeans are used for many purposes other than food consumption. Products of soybeans are used in linoleum, enamels, candles, celluloid, rubber substitutes, printing ink, lubrication, glue, fertilizer, paper sizing, soap stock and others.

Soybeans are an excellent meat substitute because they contain up to 40 percent protein. They are rich in vitamin B and contain many minerals. Lecithin is an important product extracted from soybeans which has been used to reduce blood cholesterol. Lecithin acts as a homogenizing agent which breaks the fat up into tiny particles of uniform size and quality. Because of its emulsifying action on fats, it is used in commercial processes such as keeping the fat from separating in chocolate candy.

Soybeans, which tend to ferment easily, are sometimes difficult to sprout, especially in hot weather. They must be flooded several times a day with lukewarm water then thoroughly drained. Only use seeds from the current year's crop.

Sprouting method	pot or jar
Temperature	68° to 86°
Rinse	every 3 hours
Harvest length	2 inches
Sprouting time	about 4 days
Yield	1 cup beans makes 4 to 5 cups sprouts

Sunflower Seeds

The botanical name of this plant, *Helianthus annunas,* comes from the Greek word, *helios,* sun, and *anthos,* flower. As the sun rises in the morning, the sunflower lifts its face to the east. Keeping its face in direct line with the sun, it follows the sun until sunset. When the sun sets the sunflower bows its head for the night, only to be lifted again when the sun rises the next morning.

Sunflowers were cultivated by the American Indians on the shores of Lake Huron. It is believed the Indians obtained the sunflower seeds from the prairies west of the Mississippi. The sunflower stalk provided the Indians with textile fiber, the leaves provided fodder and the flowers were a source of dye. The seeds were valued for food and hair oil.

The sunflower was a sacred symbol to the Incas, who worshipped it as a representation of the sun. In China, a fabric is made from the fiber of the stalk. Russia uses the seeds for food and oil. The Russians also grind the seeds into oil cakes, which are used for fodder for their stock.

Sunflower seeds are quick and easy to sprout. Do not over-sprout them as they will develop a strong flavor that burns the back of the throat when eaten. The sprouts are best when the root does not exceed the length of the seed.

Sprouting method	jar or pot
Temperature	65° to 75°
Rinse	twice a day
Harvest length	root no longer than the seed
Sprouting time	24 to 36 hours
Yield	1 cup makes 3 cups sprouts

Vegetable Seeds

Cabbage, Chinese cabbage, cauliflower, collards, kale, broccoli, Brussels sprouts, kohlrabi, mustard, turnips, beets, chard, endive, lettuce and radish seeds are covered in this section.

Cabbage is one of the most ancient cultivated vegetables. Cabbage, Chinese cabbage, cauliflower, collards, kale, broccoli, Brussels sprouts, kohlrabi, mustard and turnips are all descendants of *Brassica oleraces,* a wild mustard-like weed found mostly along European sea-coasts. Today's "cabbage family" bears little resemblance to its wild ancestral parent. But like the 4000 year old parent plant, they grow best in temperate climates where the weather is cool and there is a plentiful supply of moisture. The seeds of the cabbage family are small, round, and easily sprouted.

Chinese cabbage (*pets'al*) is one of the latest additions to the cabbage family in the Western world. It is also called celery cabbage. The Chinese variety has crisp leaves and a mild cabbage flavor.

Cauliflower has been a favorite vegetable in Italy for centuries. Its name means "cabbage flower." It is native to Asia and Europe and has been cultivated since 600 B.C. Cauliflower has been much improved over the centuries and the flower has increased in size by careful cultivation.

Collards and kale are similar, except for the shape of their leaves. They were developed in the Mediterranean and Asia Minor. The Greeks and the Romans both cultivated collards and kale. England adopted them from the Romans and for thousands of years grew them as a major winter vegetable. Kale is also known as borecole. Borecole probably came from the Dutch word *boerenkool* which means "peasant cabbage." Because it is often grown in the winter, kale has been called winter greens.

Broccoli has been grown by the Greeks and the Romans for 2000 years, although it was not known in the United States until the 1920's. Broccoli was introduced as a "new" vegetable and took only 10 years to become an American favorite. Today more than 100 million pounds are produced in the United States.

Brussels sprouts are named for the capital of Belgium, where they have been cultivated for hundreds of years. Climate is a critical factor in growing Brussels sprouts. It will not develop miniature cabbage heads if the temperature rises above 55 degrees. About 85 percent of the Brussels sprouts grown in the United States are cultivated in San Mateo, Santa Cruz and Monterey counties of California where a coastal fog insures cool temperatures.

Kohlrabi has a German name. *Kohl* means cabbage and *rabi* means turnip. It is one of the few vegetables to originate in Northern Europe. Its flavor resembles a turnip, but is milder. The globe of this unusual looking plant is usually eaten and the leaves discarded.

Mustard originated in the Middle East where it has been under cultivation for over two millennia. It is often mentioned in Biblical, Greek and Roman writings. Hippocrates wrote of its medicinal qualities. Mustard was prepared in the form of a condiment by Mrs. Clements of Durham County England. It is said that she made a small fortune by selling powdered mustard. Today powdered mustard is still known as Durham mustard in England.

Turnips were once believed to be native to Russia and Scandinavia, but they were cultivated in India long before being introduced into Europe. The Romans cultivated many kinds of turnips; round, long and flat. Today's varieties may weigh as little as a few ounces to as much as 25 pounds. In the 17th century, turnips were used in England as a forage crop. The British planted turnips for crop rotation, thus providing a supply of winter food for cattle and sheep. Turnips have been highly regarded for centuries as a staple winter vegetable where no other produce was available. They were not cultivated in the United States until the early 1600's.

Beets, chard and sugar beets are from the Beta family. All three were developed from a wild species that was common in Southern Europe. The wild plant grew in sandy soil along the sea. Chard is similar to an ancient variety grown in prehistoric times. It is disease free and seldom bothered by insects. For this reason beets and chard are favorites of home gardeners.

Endive originated as an herb growing wild in Southern Europe and the Near East. The ancient Egyptians and Greeks used endive as a vegetable. It is an excellent salad plant similar to lettuce with a somewhat bitter flavor.

Modern lettuce was probably derived from the prickly wild species of the family Compositae, native to Asia Minor and adjacent areas. It gets it name, *Lactuca sative,* from an Old French word *Laitues* (milky) because of its milky root. Lettuce was served to the kings of Persia over 2500 years ago. Columbus is credited with bringing lettuce to the New World. It is now one of the most universally popular salad plants.

Radishes are also an ancient vegetable. They are believed to be native to China, where they were cultivated in the 7th century B.C. The early Egyptians also enjoyed their flavor. The ancient Greeks enjoyed pelting unpopular politicians with radishes. Radishes come in a large variety of sizes and colors, from shades of white, pink and red to purple and black. The American or European variety may weigh as little as a few grams, while the *dikon* from Japan often weighs as much as two pounds. Radishes are swift to mature: some are ready to harvest just ten days after planting.

Vegetable seed sprouts are abundant in vitamins and minerals. They are low in calories and easily digested. Vegetable sprouts are a good source of phosphorus, iron and potassium, and are rich in riboflavin, niacin, vitamin C and vitamin A. To make the best use of these succulent little plants, eat them raw in salads or add them to soups just before serving.

Sprouting method	jar
Temperature	68° to 86°
Rinse	twice a day
Harvest length	1 to 2 inches greened
Sprouting time	3 to 5 days
Yield	varies with the seed 1 T makes from 1 to 2 cups

Wheat

Wheat is the world's most widely cultivated food plant. More than 1000 million human beings eat wheat daily in various forms. Its protein and calorie contribution to man is larger than that of any other food. Since the beginning of the present century, wheat production has more than doubled.

Wheat compares favorably with other cereals in nutritive value. Hard wheat contains more protein than any other cereal except oats. The wheat grains have a relatively high content of thiamine and niacin. Wheat contains little fat, and is rich in vitamin E. Although wheat contains little vitamin C, it is increased 600 percent during early sprouting. Vitamin E, niacin and pathothenic acid are also increased during the sprouting process.

Wheat grains are easily sprouted and there is a wide variety of ways to use wheat sprouts. Breads, cakes, cookies, soups and salads are only a few. The fuzz that appears on the tiny rootlets, particularly on grain sprouts, is not mold but small feeler roots of the sprout. They are also edible.

Sprouting method	jar or flower pot
Temperature	70° to 80°
Rinse	2 or 3 times a day
Harvest length	when roots are about ½ inch
Sprouting time	about 3 or 4 days
Yield	1 cup makes 3½ to 4 cups sprouts

RECIPES

BREAKFAST

ALFALFA OMELET

6 egg whites, beaten stiff
6 egg yolks, lightly beaten
¼ cup milk or light cream
½ t salt
½ cup grated Cheddar cheese
1 cup *alfalfa sprouts*
1½ T butter

Mix egg yolks, milk, salt and cheese. Fold egg whites and sprouts into egg yolk mixture. Melt butter in a very large frying pan. Pour all of omelet mixture into the pan, cover and cook over low heat until firm. Fold omelet over and with two pancake turners, gently lift out onto a hot platter. Serves 4.

BREAKFAST RICE

2   cups *rice sprouts*
¾   cup milk
1   cup raisins
¼   t cinnamon (optional)
1   T butter
¼   cup chopped nuts
pure maple syrup

Put rice, raisins, cinnamon and milk into a saucepan; cover and cook over low heat until done, about 30 minutes. Stir in butter and pour into individual bowls. Top with pure maple syrup and sprinkle with nuts. Serves 4.

SUNFLOWER BREAKFAST

1 ripe banana
2 T honey
3 apples, grated
3 T lemon juice
1 cup *sunflower seed sprouts*
1 cup *wheat sprouts*
½ cup wheat germ
½ cup light cream
chopped almonds

In a large bowl, mash and whip banana with honey. Grate apples into the bowl and add lemon juice. Mix well and fold in sprouts, wheat germ and light cream. Serve in individual bowls and top with chopped almonds. Makes 4 generous servings.

Variation: For lower calories, omit the light cream and honey. For a special breakfast treat, omit the light cream and fold in whipped cream just before serving.

WHOLE-WHEAT PANCAKES

1 cup *wheat sprouts*
¾ cup milk
4 egg yolks
4 egg whites, beaten stiff
2 t honey
3 T corn oil
½ t salt
1 cup whole-wheat flour
2 t baking powder
2 T corn starch

Place wheat sprouts and ½ cup milk into an electric blender and blend 1 minute or until smooth. Add egg yolks, honey, oil and rest of milk. Mix well. Sift flour, corn starch, baking powder and salt together into a large mixing bowl. Add sprout mixture, mixing only until moistened. Fold in beaten egg whites. Bake on a preheated, lightly oiled griddle. Serve with pure maple syrup or honey. Makes 4 servings.

WHOLE-WHEAT WAFFLES

¼ cup lukewarm water
2 T dry yeast
2 cups lukewarm milk
¼ cup oil
½ t salt
1½ cups *wheat sprouts,* ground
1 t honey
2 cups whole-wheat pastry flour
2 eggs, lightly beaten

In a large mixing bowl, dissolve yeast in warm water. Let stand 5 minutes in a warm place. Add milk, oil, salt, sprouts and honey. Blend in flour and eggs. Set the mixture in a warm place until it begins to rise, about 15 minutes. Cook in a preheated, oiled waffle iron. Makes 4 large waffles.

SUNDAE BREAKFAST

2 cups *rye sprouts*
1 cup *sunflower seed sprouts*
3 ripe bananas, thinly sliced
½ cup currants or raisins
¼ cup pine nuts
½ cup yogurt
1 T honey
2 apples, grated
chopped filberts or almonds

In a bowl, combine sprouts, bananas, currants and pine nuts. In a small bowl, whip yogurt and honey until well blended, then stir in grated apples. Spoon sprout and banana mixture into individual bowls. Top with yogurt mixture and sprinkle with chopped nuts. Makes 4 to 6 servings.

APPETIZERS

CHIVE ROUNDS

8 oz. cream cheese
½ cup chopped chives
1 t French mustard
½ t salt
½ t freshly ground pepper
½ cup *fenugreek* or *chia sprouts,*
   chopped

Cream the cheese together with mustard, salt and pepper. Add chives and sprouts. Shape into a long log. Chill. Slice into rounds

SWISS EGGS

6 eggs, hard cooked
2 T soft butter
¼ cup grated Swiss cheese
½ cup *cress, alfalfa* or *chia sprouts*

Cut eggs in half length-wise. Cream egg yolks with butter and grated cheese. Add sprouts, mix well and fill egg white halves. Garnish with paprika or a sprinkle of sprouts. Makes 12 halves.

AVOCADO CUCUMBERS

2 cucumbers
1 small avocado
1 green onion, finely chopped
dash Tabasco
1 T lemon juice
salt
6 cherry tomatoes, thinly sliced
1 cup *alfalfa sprouts,* chopped

Slice unpeeled cucumbers diagonally across, about ½-inch thick. Let slices drain on a paper towel a few minutes. Mash avocado with a fork and whip until creamy. Add lemon juice, green onion, Tabasco sauce, alfalfa sprouts and salt. Mix well. Spread cucumber slices with avocado mixture and top with a slice of tomato.

STUFFED TOMATOES

1 box cherry tomatoes
½ cup *alfalfa sprouts,* chopped
¼ cup *lentil sprouts,* chopped
¼ cup *mung bean sprouts,* chopped
1 T minced chives
2 T oil
1 T lemon juice
salt and pepper

Wash tomatoes and remove a small slice from the top. Scoop out centers with a small vegetable scoop. Sieve pulp into a bowl and add remaining ingredients. Mix well. Fill tomatoes with mixture. Chill until ready to serve.

STUFFED MUSHROOMS

12 raw mushrooms, stemmed
½ cup grated cheese
2 t minced onion
2 T finely chopped celery
½ cup chopped *bean* or *alfalfa sprouts*

Mix cheese, onion, celery and sprouts. Fill cavity of mushrooms with mixture. Sprinkle tops with alfalfa sprouts. Makes 12.

MUSHROOM SPREAD

1 cup chopped mushrooms or
  mushroom stems
2 T butter
1 T finely chopped chives
1 T finely chopped parsley
1 cup *mung bean sprouts,* chopped
½ t salt
2 t corn starch
2-3 T water

Saute mushrooms with butter until golden brown. Add all other ingredients and cook, stirring until mixture thickens. Spread on buttered whole-wheat toast. Cut in small squares and serve immediately. This spread is excellent served on vegetable wedges. Makes about 1½ cups.

CUCUMBER SPREAD

1 cucumber
2 T chopped chives or grated onion
8 oz. cream cheese
1 t salt
½ cup *fenugreek sprouts,* chopped

Cut unpeeled cucumber in half lengthwise. Scoop out seeds and center pulp. Grate remaining cucumber on a coarse shredder. Drain grated cucumber and mix with remaining ingredients. Use on crackers or in sandwiches. Makes about 2 cups.

COTTAGE CHEESE DIP

1 cup cottage cheese
¼ t caraway seeds
1 clove garlic, pressed
¼ cup yogurt
½ cup *fenugreek sprouts,* finely
   chopped
salt

Force cottage cheese through a sieve. Add remaining ingredients. Chill 2 hours. Makes 1½ cups.

VERDE DIP

8 oz. cream cheese
¾ cup finely chopped *cress sprouts*
½ cup yogurt
1 T finely chopped chives
2 t tarragon
2 T finely chopped parsley
½ t chervil
¼ t dill
salt

Cream yogurt and cheese until smooth. Add other ingredients and mix well. Refrigerate at least 2 hours before serving. Makes about 1¾ cups.

CHEESE BALLS

8 oz. cream cheese
¼ cup grated cheese
½ t salt
1 t minced onion
1 cup *alfalfa sprouts*
½ cup *wheat sprouts*
toasted wheat germ

Cream together all ingredients except wheat germ. Form into small balls and roll in wheat germ until covered. Chill until ready to serve.

WHEAT BALLS

½ cup cream cheese
1 cup *sprouted wheat*
1 cup chopped nuts
1 cup raisins
wheat germ or sesame seeds

Mix all ingredients until well blended. Shape into bite-sized balls and roll in toasted wheat germ or sesame seeds.

CHILI PUFFS

1 4 oz. can green chilies, finely
    chopped
1 t chili powder
dash cayenne
½ clove garlic, pressed (optional)
1 cup *lentil sprouts*
½ t salt
1 cup grated cheese
¾ cup mayonnaise
bread, thinly sliced

In a bowl, mix chilies, chili powder, cayenne, garlic, salt and sprouts. In another bowl, combine mayonnaise and grated cheese. Cover bread with a layer of the chili mixture. Top with the cheese and mayonnaise mixture. Broil until puffy and lightly browned. Cut into small shapes.

PARMESAN PUFFS

½ cup grated Parmesan cheese
¾ cup mayonnaise
French bread, sliced
1 small red onion, thinly sliced
1 cup *alfalfa sprouts*
butter

Spread bread lightly with butter. Mix mayonnaise and Parmesan cheese. Place a layer of onion slices on bread and cover with Parmesan spread. Broil until cheese melts and is lightly browned. Top with a mound of sprouts.

SOUPS

WATERCRESS SOUP

2 T butter
2 T minced onion
3 cups milk
3 cups water
1 bunch watercress
1 t salt
1 cup *buckwheat sprouts*

In a saucepan, saute onions in butter until transparent. Put remaining ingredients in a blender and blend until smooth. Add blended mixture to sauteed onions, bring to boiling point and cook over low heat for 5 minutes. Serves 6 to 8.

CREAM OF FENUGREEK SOUP

2 cups *fenugreek sprouts*
1 large potato
1½ cups potato water
1 cup milk
salt

Scrub potato and cook in skin until tender. Remove skin and chop potato. Put fenugreek sprouts, chopped potato and milk in a blender. Blend until smooth and pour into a saucepan; add 1½ cups of the potato water. Season to taste. Heat soup just to boiling point and serve at once. Makes 4 servings.

SOY VEGETABLE SOUP

4 cups water
1 cup fresh peas or *pea sprouts*
1 cup finely chopped celery
½ cup grated carrots
½ cup diced turnips
1 onion, finely chopped
2 cups coarsely ground *soybean
   sprouts*
1 t salt
2 t powdered vegetable broth
minced parsley

Put all ingredients, except salt, in a large saucepan. Cover and cook over low heat for 20 minutes. Add salt and garnish with minced parsley. Makes 4 to 6 servings.

CREAM OF SOY SOUP

3 cups *soybean sprouts*
½ cup water
3 cups milk
salt to taste
chopped *alfalfa sprouts*

Put soybean sprouts and water in a saucepan, cook over low heat for 15 minutes or until tender. Force the beans through a sieve or whirl in a blender until smooth. Heat milk in the saucepan and add soybean puree. Salt to taste and serve hot, topped with chopped alfalfa sprouts. Serves 4.

CHIA TOMATO SOUP

5 large tomatoes, peeled and chopped
2 T butter
½ bay leaf
⅛ t thyme
2 whole cloves
2 thin slices onion
1½ cups water
1 T cornstarch
¾ t salt
4 T grated Parmesan cheese
½ cup *chia sprouts*, tops and stems only.

Harvest chia sprouts by snipping close to the root with scissors. Put tomatoes, herbs, cloves, onion and butter in a saucepan and cook over low heat for 12 minutes. Remove cloves and bay leaf. Force tomatoes through a sieve; add water and cornstarch. Stir and cook until slightly thickened. Add salt and chia sprouts; reheat. Serve hot and top each serving with a spoonful of cheese. Makes 4 servings.

Variation: Omit *chia sprouts* and use 1 cup of *alfalfa sprouts*.

LENTIL SOUP

2 T butter
1 onion, finely chopped
1 carrot, grated
2 stalks celery, finely chopped
3 large tomatoes, chopped
1 T tomato paste
4 cups *lentil sprouts*
3 cups vegetable or beef stock
1½ t salt
¼ t pepper

Heat butter in a saucepan, add onions and saute about 3 minutes. Add carrots, celery, tomatoes, tomato paste, lentils and stock. Cover and cook over low heat for 20 minutes. Add salt and pepper and continue to cook for 3 minutes more. Serves 4 to 6.

Variation: Saute ¼ pound beef, (cut into ¼-inch cubes) with onions, then add other ingredients.

GREEN PEA SOUP

4 cups vegetable or meat stock
3 cups *green pea sprouts*
1 onion, chopped
2 T minced parsley
1 t chopped mint
1 clove garlic, chopped
1 small head lettuce, chopped
1 t salt
pepper

Put peas, onions, lettuce, parsley, garlic and mint in a large saucepan. Add 1 cup of vegetable stock. Cover and simmer for 30 minutes. Press vegetables through a sieve. Heat remaining stock, then stir in the vegetable puree and seasonings. Simmer for 5 minutes. Serve with croutons. Makes 4 servings.

MILLET SOUP

1 T sesame oil
½ cup chopped onion
1 cup banana squash, cut in ½" cubes
2 cups *millet sprouts*
4 cups hot water
1 T soy sauce

Heat oil in a saucepan and sauté the onion until transparent. Add squash and cook two minutes longer. Add millet sprouts, water and soy sauce. Cover and simmer 30 minutes. Makes 4 servings.

BLACK BEAN SOUP

4 cups *black bean sprouts*
1 clove garlic
1 onion, chopped
1 green pepper, chopped
3 T olive oil
½ t cumin
1 t oregano
4 cups water or stock
1 t salt

Saute garlic, onion and pepper in oil until tender. Add sprouts, cumin, oregano and 2 cups water or stock. Cook 30 minutes. Pour into a blender and blend until smooth. Heat remaining 2 cups water in a saucepan, add blended beans and salt. Reheat. Serves 4 to 6.

NAVY BEAN SOUP

4 cups *navy bean sprouts*
2 cups vegetable or meat broth
1 large onion, chopped
2 cloves garlic, minced
½ t rosemary
½ t caraway seeds
2 T tomato paste
1 bay leaf
salt
pepper
2 T margarine or butter

Simmer all ingredients except salt, pepper and margarine, until tender, about 30 minutes. Remove bay leaf and add salt, pepper and margarine. Place in a blender and liquify for 30 seconds. Makes 5 servings.

GAZPACHO VERDE

6 green tomatoes
1 green pepper, chopped
1 unpeeled cucumber, diced
¼ cup olive oil
1 clove garlic, minced
½ t salt
2 T vinegar
⅛ t cumin
1½ cups chopped *alfalfa sprouts*
1 T grated onion
¾ cup iced water
½ cup dry white wine

Scald tomatoes with boiling water. Remove skins, then cut in quarters. Finely grind tomatoes, green peppers and cucumbers. Put olive oil, garlic, salt, vinegar and cumin in a blender and mix about 1 minute. In a large mixing bowl, combine ground vegetables, alfalfa sprouts, grated onions and olive oil mixture. Chill thoroughly. Just before serving, blend in iced water and wine to desired consistency. Serve plain or garnish with chopped red tomatoes, croutons or chopped hard-cooked eggs. Makes 4 to 6 servings.

GAZPACHO ROJO

2 cups dry white wine
1 t coriander seeds, bruised
½ t black peppercorns, bruised
1 T chopped fresh basil or
1 t dried basil
2 large bay leaves
½ t finely chopped garlic
6 cups chicken stock
2 t lemon juice
2 lbs. ripe tomatoes, peeled, seeded and chopped
2 small cucumbers, seeded and diced
⅓ cup chopped celery
¾ cup chopped green peppers
4 T chopped green onions
2 T finely chopped parsley
1 T dried dill weed
salt
freshly ground pepper
2 cups *chopped alfalfa sprouts*
⅔ cup olive oil

Mix all ingredients. Chill and serve with garlic croutons. Serves 8.

SALADS

WATERCRESS CHEESE SALAD

2 bunches watercress
1 cup *sunflower seed sprouts*
1 bunch parsley, chopped
¼ lb. Monterey or Swiss cheese
1 large tomato, chopped
oil and lemon dressing
salt

Wash and drain watercress, then break into small pieces, discarding large stems. Cut cheese into small cubes. Combine all ingredients in a large bowl and toss lightly with oil and lemon or vinegar dressing. Season to taste. Makes 4 servings.

CRISPY CRUNCHY SALAD

2 large tomatoes
1 cup *alfalfa sprouts*
1 cup *wheat sprouts*
1 cup *mung bean sprouts*
1 cup *sunflower seed sprouts*
3 T oil, olive or sesame
2 T lemon juice or vinegar
salt and pepper

Mix tomatoes and sprouts in a large bowl. Pour over oil and toss until sprouts are evenly coated. Add lemon juice and seasonings, toss lightly and serve immediately. Serves 4 to 6.

TOMATO TUBS

3 large tomatoes
1½ cups *alfalfa sprouts*
2 T chopped green onions
1 medium avocado, chopped
1 T lemon juice
1 T salad oil
dash cayenne
salt
lettuce

Wash and stem tomatoes and cut in half lengthwise. Scoop out pulp and place in a blender. Add onions, avocado, lemon juice, salt, oil and cayenne. Blend 10 seconds, pour into a bowl and fold in alfalfa sprouts. On individual salad plates, place each tomato half on a bed of lettuce. Fill tomato halves with alfalfa mixture and garnish with a sprinkle of alfalfa sprouts.

WHOLE EARTH SALAD

1 cup *alfalfa sprouts*
1 cup *mung bean sprouts*
1 cup *adzuki sprouts*
½ cup *rye sprouts*
½ cup *lentil sprouts*
1 cup cubed cheese
1 bunch watercress, broken
1 head romaine lettuce, broken
¼ cup finely chopped bell pepper
¼ cup chopped green onions
2 T minced parsley
2 large tomatoes, chopped
1 large avocado, chopped

Put all ingredients in a large salad bowl, toss lightly with oil and vinegar dressing. Serves 8 generously.

ADZUKI SPROUT SALAD

2 cups *adzuki bean sprouts*
2 T water
1½ cups chopped celery
6 radishes, thinly sliced
1 cucumber, diced
½ cup finely chopped green pepper
1 cup shredded lettuce

Put sprouts into a saucepan with water and steam 2 minutes. Cool, then mix with other ingredients. Chill and serve topped with French dressing. Serves 4.

FRENCH DRESSING

1½ cups oil, olive, sesame or corn
1 clove garlic, crushed
1 T minced onion
1 t caraway seeds
½ cup lemon juice
1½ t salt
pepper
dash paprika
½ t dried tarragon

Mix all ingredients and refrigerate in covered jar until ready to use. Makes 2 cups.

MUNG BEAN SALAD

1 cup *mung bean sprouts*
1 cup finely chopped celery
1 cup grated carrots
½ cup chopped cashew or pine nuts
1 T sesame seeds
French dressing
water cress or lettuce

Combine sprouts, celery, grated carrots, nuts and sesame seeds. Add French dressing and toss lightly. Serve on a bed of watercress or lettuce. Serves 4.

LENTIL SPROUT SALAD

2 cups *lentil sprouts*
1 tomato, chopped
3 T oil
1 T wine vinegar
1 T minced onion
½ t curry powder

Mix oil, vinegar, minced onion, and curry powder. Let stand 30 minutes. Combine lentil sprouts and chopped tomato. Pour curry dressing over salad and toss lightly. Season with salt and pepper if desired. Serves 4.

BEAN SPROUT TOMATO SALAD

1 head butter (Boston) lettuce
1 cucumber, thinly sliced
3 tomatoes, sliced
2 cups *bean sprouts,* any kind
6 - 8 radishes, sliced
ripe olives

Place lettuce leaves on salad plates, then a layer of bean sprouts. Place alternate layers of sliced cucumbers, radishes and tomatoes over the bean sprouts, creating a pyramid. Top with sour cream dressing and garnish with ripe olives. Serves 6.

SOUR CREAM DRESSING

½ cup sour cream
1½ T finely chopped chives
1 T vinegar or lemon juice
¼ t salt

Mix all ingredients thoroughly. Makes ½ cup.

ALFALFA SPROUT TOSS

2 cups finely chopped celery
1 cup *alfalfa sprouts*
1 cup currants
2 carrots, grated

Mix ingredients thoroughly and chill until ready to serve. Serve on individual salad plates topped with yogurt dressing. Serves 4 to 6.

YOGURT DRESSING

¾ cup yogurt
¼ cup mayonnaise
1 t mustard
½ t salt

Mix all ingredients and chill until ready to use. Makes 1 cup.

ORIENTAL SALAD

1 cup cooked shrimp
1 cup cooked scallops or crab
2 cups *mung bean sprouts*
1 cup chow mein noodles
1 5 oz. can water chestnuts, chopped
¼ cup minced green onions
¼ cup finely chopped celery
¾ cup mayonnaise
1 T soy sauce
1 T lemon juice
¾ t powdered ginger
lettuce leaves

For the dressing, mix mayonnaise, soy sauce, lemon juice and ginger. Mix remaining ingredients, except lettuce. Toss salad with dressing and serve on lettuce leaves. Serves 6.

SESAME SALAD

1 cup watercress
1 cup torn lettuce
1 cup *sunflower seed sprouts*
1 cup *alfalfa sprouts*

Mix all ingredients in a large bowl and toss with Sesame Dressing.

FRESH MUSHROOM SALAD

1 cup sliced raw mushrooms
1 small potato, scrubbed and thinly sliced
1 cup *bean sprouts*, any kind
2 cups *alfalfa sprouts*
½ cup fresh peas
Sesame Dressing

Mix all ingredients in a large bowl and chill until ready to serve. Serve with Sesame Dressing or any oil base dressing. Serves 4.

SESAME DRESSING

¼ cup ground sesame seeds
½ cup water
¼ t kelp
2 T lemon juice
¼ small garlic clove

Blend in electric blender until smooth. Makes about ½ cup.

AVOCADO SHRIMP ASPIC

1 T unflavored gelatin
¾ cup boiling water
2 T honey
1 T Worcestershire sauce
1 T vinegar
¼ cup lemon juice
1 cup tomato sauce
2 t grated onion
1 cup chopped celery
1 8 oz. can shrimp
1 avocado, chopped
1 cup *alfalfa sprouts*

Dissolve gelatin and honey in hot water. Cool to room temperature and add all other ingredients except avocado and sprouts. Mix well, then fold in alfalfa sprouts and avocado. Pour into mold and chill in refrigerator until set. Unmold and serve on a bed of lettuce. Serves 6.

Vegetarian variation: Omit the shrimp and add another chopped avocado.

ALFALFA CABBAGE MOLD

1 envelope unflavored gelatin
½ cup cold water
2 cups boiling water
1 lemon, juiced
3 T honey
1 cup finely shredded cabbage
1 cup finely chopped celery
¼ cup finely chopped green pepper
1 cup *alfalfa sprouts*

Soak gelatin in cold water for 5 minutes. Add lemon juice, boiling water, and honey. Mix well and refrigerate until mixture begins to set, then fold in remaining ingredients. Pour into a mold and refrigerate until firmly set. Unmold and serve on a bed of lettuce. Serves 6.

CABBAGE SPROUT SLAW

2 cups *alfalfa sprouts*
1 cup *cabbage sprouts,* chopped
½ cup chopped fresh pineapple or
    canned unsweetened crushed
    pineapple
½ cup seedless grapes, cut in halves
½ cup yogurt
¼ cup mayonnaise
1 t mustard
½ t salt

Combine cabbage sprouts, alfalfa
sprouts, grapes and pineapple in a
large bowl. In a small bowl, mix
yogurt, mayonnaise, mustard and
salt. Pour dressing over salad and
toss lightly. Serve on lettuce or
other salad greens. Serves 4.

WHEAT TOMATO SALAD

1 cup *wheat sprouts,* chopped
4 green onions, finely chopped
½ cup finely chopped parsley
4 sprigs fresh mint, finely chopped
    or ½ t dried mint
4 large tomatoes, finely chopped
¼ cup lemon juice
½ cup olive oil
salt and pepper to taste

Combine all ingredients and mix
well. Serve on lettuce or cabbage
leaves. Serves 6.

GARBANZO RELISH

2 cups *garbanzo sprouts*
3 green onions, minced
1 clove garlic, minced
1 large tomato, chopped
2 T chopped pimiento
¼ cup minced parsley
6 T olive oil
2 T wine vinegar
½ t salt
freshly ground pepper

Steam garbanzo sprouts until tender, about 10 minutes. Cool and combine with remaining ingredients. Refrigerate and marinate for several hours. Makes 4 to 6 servings.

FAVA BEAN SALAD

2 cloves garlic, crushed
6 T olive oil
¼ cup lemon juice
1 t salt
2 cups *fava bean sprouts*
2 green onions, chopped
1 large tomato, chopped
1 T chopped mint leaves

For the dressing, combine garlic, olive oil, lemon juice and salt. Let stand 20 minutes. Mix vegetables, sprouts and mint leaves in a bowl. Pour dressing over salad and serve at once. Makes 4 servings.

COTTAGE CHEESE SALAD

1 cup low fat cottage cheese
½ cup plain yogurt
¼ cup finely chopped radish
1 T minced onion
¼ cup finely chopped celery
⅔ cups *wheat sprouts*
salt
alfalfa sprouts or watercress

Mix cottage cheese and yogurt. Add
all remaining ingredients except alfalfa sprouts. Chill. Serve on a bed
of alfalfa sprouts or watercress.
Makes 2 luncheon-size salads.

VEGETABLES

MINTED LIMA BEAN SPROUTS

3 cups *lima bean sprouts*
½ cup hot milk
2 sprigs fresh mint, finely chopped
½ t salt
1 T butter or margarine
paprika

Put beans and milk in a saucepan, cover and simmer until tender, about 10 minutes. Add mint, salt and butter. Serve garnished with paprika. Serves 4.

CRUNCHY CABBAGE

3 T oil
4 cups shredded cabbage
2 cups *mung bean sprouts*
1 T caraway seeds
salt
pepper

Heat oil and saute cabbage and sprouts for 5 minutes or until cabbage is cooked but still crisp. Add caraway seeds, salt and pepper. Toss lightly to mix. Serves 6.

CURRIED FENUGREEK I

2 cups *fenugreek sprouts,* chopped
3 T butter
1 clove garlic, minced
¼ t cardamon
1 t turmeric
1 t mustard seed
¼ t ground cumin
¼ t cayenne
1 cup yogurt
1 T flour

In a saucepan, heat butter. Add spices and garlic. Cook over low heat until mustard seeds pop. Add fenugreek, mix well, cover and cook for 2 minutes. Mix flour with yogurt until smooth and add to fenugreek. Continue heating until mixture is hot: do not boil. Serve at once. Serves 4.

CURRIED FENUGREEK II

2 cups *fenugreek sprouts,* chopped
1 small onion, chopped
2 t curry powder or to taste
2 T oil
1 t corn starch
¼ cup warm water

In a frying pan, saute chopped onions in oil until transparent. Add curry powder and fenugreek sprouts, mix well. Dissolve corn starch in warm water and add to fenugreek sprouts. Cook until mixture thickens. Makes 4 servings.

SWISS CHARD AND LENTILS

1 tomato
2 cups *lentil sprouts*
½ lb. Swiss chard, finely chopped
¼ cup finely chopped onions
2 T butter or margarine
1 T minced parsley
1 clove garlic, finely chopped
¼ t sweet basil
½ t salt

Peel and press tomato through a sieve. Saute onions in butter until transparent. Add tomato and other ingredients. Cover and steam 5 minutes. Serves 6.

BLACK BEANS WITH RICE

3 cups *black bean sprouts*
2 cups *rice sprouts*
¾ cup water
1 large onion, finely chopped
2 cloves garlic, crushed
1 green pepper, finely chopped
1 bay leaf
1 t salt
½ t pepper
¼ cup olive oil
¼ lb. smoked ham, finely chopped

Heat 2 tablespoons olive oil in a large skillet and add half of the onion, garlic, green pepper, salt and pepper. Saute until tender, then add beans, rice, bay leaf and water. Cook covered over low heat until tender, about 30 minutes. Remove bay leaf and let mixture stand 5 minutes. Meanwhile, heat ham in remaining 2 tablespoons of olive oil. When lightly sauteed, add remaining onion, garlic, green pepper and seasonings. Continue cooking until golden brown. Serve ham mixture over beans and rice. Serves 6.

POTATOES AND FENUGREEK

1 lb. potatoes, cooked in jackets
2 T oil or margarine
½ t turmeric
2 cups *fenugreek sprouts*
dash cayenne
1 t salt

Peel and chop boiled potatoes. Heat oil in a large frying pan and add potatoes and turmeric. Saute potatoes 3 minutes, stirring constantly. Add fenugreek, cayenne and salt. Mix well and continue to cook covered for 5 minutes. Serves 4.

SPROUT TOMATO SAUCE

1 cup *mung bean sprouts*, chopped
1 large onion, finely chopped
2 T oil
½ cup chopped celery
½ cup chopped green pepper
2 cups stewed tomatoes

Saute onions in oil until lightly browned. Sieve tomatoes and add with rest of ingredients to onions. Cover and simmer 10 minutes. Serve over vegetables, meat loaf, or grain patties.

BLACK-EYED PEAS WITH HERBS

4 cups *black-eyed pea sprouts*
2 T margarine or butter
1 medium onion, chopped
1 bay leaf
½ t thyme
2 whole cloves
¼ t pepper
½ t salt
¼ cup hot water

Saute onion in margarine until transparent. Add remaining ingredients and simmer 10 minutes or until tender. Remove bay leaf and cloves before serving. Black-eyed peas are naturally delicious with corn bread. Makes 4 servings.

YELLOW PEAS IN YOGURT

2½ cups *yellow pea sprouts*
1 t dried mint
1 T butter
1 t flour
½ cup yogurt
½ t salt

Steam sprouts for 6 to 8 minutes, or until just tender. Drain, add butter and mint. Mix well. Combine flour, yogurt and salt and whip until smooth. Add yogurt to peas and reheat, do not boil. Serve immediately. Makes 4 servings.

ENTREES

ADZUKI PATTIES

1 cup *adzuki sprouts*
½ cup oatmeal
½ cup water
2 eggs, slightly beaten
¼ cup finely chopped onions
¼ t salt
oil

Soak oatmeal in water for 2 hours. Grind adzuki sprouts, using the coarse blade. Combine all ingredients and mix well. Heat a little oil in a skillet. Spoon mixture into the pan and flatten into patties with the back of the spoon. Brown lightly on both sides. Serves 2 or 3.

CHICKPEA CROQUETTES

3 cups *chickpea sprouts*
¼ cup water
1 medium potato, cooked
¼ cup chopped parsley
½ t salt
pepper
4 T olive oil

Steam sprouts in water for 10 minutes. Grind potato and chickpea sprouts. Add parsley, salt and pepper and blend well. Form into small cakes and saute in olive oil until browned on both sides. Makes about 12 small cakes.

WHEAT SPROUT PATTIES I

2 cups *wheat sprouts*
1 egg, slightly beaten
2 T minced onion
2 T minced green pepper
2 T chopped mushrooms
oil
celery salt

Grind wheat sprouts, add egg and vegetables. Mix well. Heat a little oil in a skillet. Spoon sprout mixture into the pan and press with back of spoon to form patties no more than ½-inch thick. Cook about 2 minutes on each side over medium-low heat, or until lightly browned on both sides. Sprinkle with celery salt and serve hot as a main dish or as hors d'oeuvres. Serves 4. These patties are tasty when served with Sprout Tomato Sauce.

WHEAT SPROUT PATTIES II

2 cups finely ground *wheat sprouts*
clarified butter
salt

Butter hands, then shape ground wheat sprouts into patties not more than ½-inch thick. Heat clarified butter or oil in a heavy frying pan. Saute patties over medium heat until golden brown on both sides. Sprinkle with salt and keep warm until ready to serve. Serves 3 or 4.

Variation: Use *rye sprouts* instead of *wheat sprouts*.

BUCKWHEAT NOODLES

1 cup ground *buckwheat sprouts*
1 egg, slightly beaten
¾ to 1 cup buckwheat flour
¼ t salt

Mix buckwheat sprouts, egg and salt. Add enough buckwheat flour to make a stiff dough. Cover with a cloth and let stand 15 minutes. On a floured board, roll dough as thin as possible. Let dry 1 hour, then cut into ¼ inch to ½ inch strips. Cook noodles in hot boiling water for about 8 minutes. Serves 4.

BUCKWHEAT THINS

2 cups finely ground *buckwheat sprouts*
clarified butter
salt

Form ground sprouts into ¼ inch thick patties. Heat a little butter in a heavy frying pan and saute patties until golden brown on both sides, adding butter as required. Salt lightly. Serves 2 or 3. Thins make tasty hot snacks.

FALAFEL

3 cups *fava bean sprouts*
2 T flour
½ t baking soda
1 clove garlic, finely chopped
1 egg, lightly beaten
2 T finely chopped parsley
½ t salt
¼ t pepper
¼ t cumin
1 t turmeric
¼ t basil
¼ t marjoram
1 T olive oil
¼ t cayenne
oil for deep frying

Mix all ingredients. Mixture will be soft. Form into 1 inch balls. Drop four or five at a time in oil heated to 365°. Balls will rise to surface and are light brown when cooked. Cooking time is about 2 minutes. Drain on paper towel. Serve hot or at room temperature. Yields about 30 falafel.

ALFALFA SPROUT RAREBIT

¼ cup raw cashews
1 t salt
2 cups water
1 T flour
1 t instant minced onion or
   1 T minced fresh onion
3 T corn starch
1 T butter
¼ cup sliced olives
3 T tahini (sesame paste) or raw nut
   butter
pimentos for garnish
1 T chopped chives
1½ cups *alfalfa sprouts*

Put water, cashews, salt, flour, onion and corn starch in a blender. Liquify 30 seconds, then pour into a saucepan. Heat over low fire until sauce thickens. Remove from heat and add tahini, butter, chives and alfalfa sprouts. Mix well. Reheat, do not boil. Serve over whole-wheat toast and garnish with strips of pimentos and ripe olives. Serves 4.

EGG FOO YUNG

2 onions, finely chopped
2 green peppers, finely chopped
4 eggs, slightly beaten
2 T oil
½ t salt
3 cups *mung bean sprouts*

Mix all ingredients well. Spoon onto a hot oiled grill and saute until lightly browned on both sides.

SAFFRON RICE PATTIES

⅛ t saffron, crumbled
2 cups finely ground *rice sprouts*
2 T hot water
2 eggs, slightly beaten
1 T chopped chives
½ t salt
oil or clarified butter

Pour hot water over saffron and let stand 5 minutes. Add all other ingredients except oil and mix well. Drop spoonfuls of mixture on hot oiled griddle or heavy frying pan. Brown on both sides. Serves 3 or 4. Patties are excellent when served as hot hors d'oeuvres.

ORANGE RICE

3 T butter
⅔ cup chopped celery
2 T minced onion
½ cup water
¼ cup orange juice
2 t grated orange peel
1¼ t salt
3 cups *rice sprouts*

In a heavy saucepan, saute celery and onions until just tender. Add water, orange peel, juice and salt. Bring to a boil and add rice sprouts. Cover and steam over low heat 30 minutes. Remove from heat and let stand 10 minutes. Serves 4 to 6.

PILAF

4 cups *rice sprouts,* steamed
¼ cup butter or margarine
¼ cup ground almonds
¼ cup raisins
¼ cup pine nuts
¼ t salt
¼ cup clear stock, vegetable or meat

Melt butter and saute almonds, raisins and pine nuts until golden brown, stirring constantly. Add hot stock and rice sprouts. Cover and keep warm until ready to serve. This rice dish is very tasty served with chicken or lamb chops. Serves 4 to 6.

LENTIL AND RICE SPROUTS

1 small onion, chopped
2 T butter or oil
1 cup *rice sprouts*
¾ cup water
2 cups *lentil sprouts*

Saute onion in butter until transparent; add rice sprouts and water. Cook over low heat for 10 minutes, add lentil sprouts and continue to cook for 20 minutes longer. Salt to taste. Serves 4.

CHEESE RICE BAKE

3 cups *rice sprouts,* finely ground
1 green pepper, finely chopped
1 onion, finely chopped
3 T butter or margarine
½ cup finely chopped parsley
1½ cups milk
3 eggs, beaten
2 cups grated Cheddar cheese
1½ t salt
⅛ t pepper

Saute onions and green pepper in butter until tender. Add other ingredients and pour into a baking dish. Bake in 350° oven for 1 hour. Serves 4.

LENTIL CHEESE LOAF

4 cups *lentil sprouts*
2 T melted butter
2 eggs, slightly beaten
½ t salt
¼ t thyme
¼ t black pepper
¼ cup minced green pepper
3 T minced onion
½ cup grated carrot
1 cup grated Cheddar cheese
1 cup soft whole-wheat bread crumbs

Grind lentil sprouts. Put in a mixing bowl with melted butter, salt, eggs, thyme, green pepper, onion, black pepper and carrots. Mix well. Fold in bread crumbs and grated cheese. Bake in well greased loaf pan for 45 minutes in a 350° oven. Serve plain or with a tomato sauce. Cold lentil loaf makes a tasty filling for sandwiches. Serves 4 to 6.

SPROUTS AU GRATIN

3 cups *soybean sprouts*
2 T oil
2 T flour
1 cup milk
¾ cup cottage cheese
1 t salt
¼ t pepper
¼ cup bread crumbs

Steam sprouts for 10 minutes. Heat oil over medium heat and stir in flour. Add milk gradually, stirring constantly until mixture boils and thickens. Add ½ cup cheese and seasonings. Stir until cheese melts. Add sprouts and mix well. Pour into a greased casserole. Sprinkle with the rest of the cheese and top with bread crumbs, then dot with butter. Bake in 375° oven for 30 minutes or until brown. Serves 4 to 6.

ALFA-CHEESE TORTILLAS

1 doz. corn tortillas
1 lb. Cheddar cheese, grated
½ cup sour cream or yogurt
2 cups *alfalfa sprouts*
margarine

Spread a thin coat of margarine over one side of the corn tortillas. Heat a heavy frying pan or grill over medium heat. Put a tortilla in the pan, margarine side down. Sprinkle the top with grated cheese, then dot with sour cream or yogurt. When cheese has melted, remove tortilla to hot platter, sprinkle alfalfa sprouts liberally over melted cheese, then roll up into a tube. Repeat for each tortilla. Keep platter in warm oven until all tortillas are prepared. Serve immediately. Makes 1 dozen tortillas.

VEGETABLE CHEESE CASSEROLE

1½ cups *pea sprouts*
1 onion, finely chopped
1½ cups *mung bean sprouts*
¼ cup finely chopped pimento
¼ cup grated carrot
2 T finely chopped parsley
1 cup white sauce (medium thick)
1 cup grated cheese
¼ cup dry bread crumbs

Blend all ingredients except bread crumbs. Pour into a casserole dish, sprinkle with bread crumbs and dot with butter. Bake in 325° oven for 35 to 45 minutes. Serves 4.

VEGETARIAN CHOP SUEY

½ cup oil
2 large green peppers, cut
  in strips or cubes
1 cup chopped celery
3 green onions, chopped
1 cup boiling water
½ cup sliced mushrooms
2 cups *mung bean sprouts*
2 T cornstarch
1½ t salt
pepper
1 T soy sauce
½ cup sliced water chestnuts

Heat oil in a large skillet; saute green peppers, green onions and celery for 2 minutes. Add boiling water; cover and cook 7 minutes. Make a paste of the cornstarch, soy sauce and a little water. Add mushrooms, mung bean sprouts, salt and pepper to vegetables. Stirring constantly, add cornstarch mixture and cook until sauce thickens. Add water chestnuts and reheat. Serve piping hot over noodles or rice. Makes 4 servings.

MILLET CASSEROLE

1 onion, chopped
2 T oil
2 stalks celery, finely chopped
1½ cups finely chopped mushrooms
1 T flour
1 cup water or vegetable stock
1 t salt
⅛ t pepper
1 cup ground almonds or filberts
1 cup *sunflower seed sprouts*
2 cups *millet sprouts*

In a large frying pan, saute onions in oil until transparent. Add mushrooms and celery; cook over medium heat 3 or 4 minutes. Remove from heat and sprinkle with flour, stir until smooth, then add water, salt and pepper. Cook until thickened, stirring constantly. Remove from heat and add ground nuts, sunflower and millet sprouts. Mix well. Pour into an oiled casserole dish. Bake in 300° oven for 1 hour. Serves 4.

MINESTRONE

1 cup *red bean sprouts*
1 cup *white* or *navy bean sprouts*
1 cup *lentil sprouts*
1 cup *pea sprouts*
1 potato, diced
2 carrots, diced
½ cup chopped cabbage
1 cup chopped spinach or chard
1 T parsley
2 small zucchini, chopped
1 qt. water
1 cup whole-wheat spaghetti
¼ t sweet basil
¼ cup olive oil
2 cloves garlic, chopped
dash of cloves

In a large pot, combine sprouts, vegetables, spaghetti and water. Cook until tender, about 15 to 20 minutes. Make a paste of ¼ teaspoon sweet basil, garlic, olive oil and a dash of cloves. Add to soup. Serve with Parmesan cheese. Serves 6.

LEGUME BURGERS

1 cup *adzuki sprouts,* finely chopped
½ cup *mung bean sprouts,* finely chopped
1 cup *lentil sprouts,* finely chopped
½ cup *chickpea sprouts,* finely chopped
1 t salt
2 T oil
2 green onions, finely chopped
2 eggs, slightly beaten
¼ cup milk
½ cup soy flour

Mix all ingredients and drop large spoonfuls into a hot oiled skillet. Brown lightly on each side and serve piping hot. Serves 4.

STUFFED EGGPLANT

2 eggplants
1 red bell pepper
4 T olive oil
1 clove garlic minced
1 onion, finely chopped
1 T minced parsley
½ t basil
2 cups *fenugreek sprouts*
2 large tomatoes, chopped
salt
1 cup ground walnuts
½ cup wheat germ
¾ cup grated Parmesan cheese
2 T melted butter
1 cup light cream or milk

Slice eggplant in half lengthwise; scoop out and dice centers, leaving ¼ inch shells. Heat oil in a large skillet, add onions and saute until transparent. Add eggplant, pepper, garlic, parsley, basil, sprouts, tomato and salt to onions. Cook over medium heat until vegetables are soft. Fill and press mixture into halves. Combine ground nuts, wheat germ and cheese; moisten with melted butter and enough milk to make a soft paste. Spread mixture evenly over eggplant. Bake in 350° oven about 45 minutes. Serve piping hot. Serves 6.

OXTAIL STEW

2 lbs. oxtails, cut in chunks
1 cup water
4 T olive oil
2 carrots, sliced
2 turnips, sliced
3 onions, chopped
1 zucchini, sliced
1 bell pepper, chopped
1 tomato, chopped
2 t chili powder
1 t salt
1 t pepper
2 cups *lentil sprouts*
1 cup red wine

Heat oil in a deep frying pan and braise oxtails. Add water, cover and cook until tender. Add remaining ingredients and simmer about 15 minutes or until vegetables are tender. Makes 6 servings.

Vegetarian variation: Omit oxtails and ½ cup of water. Add 1 tablespoon unsalted, powdered vegetable broth.

CURRY SAUCE

½ cup minced onion
2 T butter
1-2 T curry powder
1 cup chicken broth
2 egg yolks
½ cup light cream
4 cups *lentil sprouts*

Saute onions in butter until transparent; add curry powder and stir well. Cook 2 minutes, then transfer sauteed onions to the top of a double boiler. Add chicken broth, cover and simmer 10 minutes over low heat. After curry broth has cooked for 5 minutes, put the lentil sprouts in a saucepan with ½ cup chicken broth and simmer 5 minutes. Whip egg yolks and cream with a fork and add ½ cup of hot curry broth. Stir egg mixture into remainder of curry broth. Cook over hot water, stirring constantly until mixture thickens. Arrange hot lentil sprouts around the chicken pieces. Spoon curry sauce over the chicken and serve immediately. Makes 4 portions.

CURRIED CHICKEN WITH LENTIL SPROUTS

3 lb. fryer chicken, disjointed
2 T butter
1 carrot, chopped
1 stalk celery, chopped
1 t salt
2 cups boiling water

In a large frying pan, brown chicken in butter. Add vegetables, salt, and boiling water; cover and simmer until tender. Lift out chicken. When cool enough to handle, remove the chicken bones, keeping the flesh in large pieces. Put chicken on a platter and spoon over 2 tablespoons of broth to keep it moist. Place in a warm oven until ready to use.

CREAMED CHICKEN ON TOAST

2 cups diced cooked chicken
1½ cup milk, warmed
1 T oil
1 T flour
¼ t salt
1 cup fresh or frozen green peas, cooked
1 cup diced fresh carrots, cooked
1½ cups *mung bean sprouts*

Heat oil in a saucepan, add flour and stir until smooth. Add warmed milk and other ingredients. Cook over low heat until mixture thickens. Serve at once over whole-wheat toast. Serves 4.

BEAN SPROUT CREOLE

1 cup finely chopped celery
1 onion, finely chopped
1 clove garlic
1 T oil
3 cups *soybean sprouts*
1 large can tomatoes
1 t salt
2 bay leaves

Heat oil in a large skillet; add celery, onion and garlic. Saute over low heat until lightly browned. Add sprouts, tomatoes, salt and bay leaves. Simmer 10 minutes. Remove bay leaves. Serve hot or cold. Makes 4 servings.

BREADS

For baking, only use grain sprouts with roots that are about one-fourth the length of the grain. Long-rooted sprouts tend to produce soggy baked goods.

WHOLE WHEAT BISCUITS

2 cups sifted whole wheat flour
4 t baking powder
½ t salt
¼ cup oil
1 cup *wheat sprouts,* ground
1 cup milk

Sift together flour, baking powder and salt. Add remaining ingredients and mix just enough to moisten dry ingredients. Put dough on a floured surface and press out to ¾-inch thickness. Cut with a 2-inch biscuit cutter. Place on an oiled baking sheet and bake 20 minutes in 450° oven. Makes about 20 biscuits.

BACON MUFFINS

2 cups whole wheat pastry flour
3 t baking powder
½ t salt
1 egg, slightly beaten
1 cup milk
¼ cup melted butter
1 cup *wheat sprouts,* ground
3 T cooked, crumbled bacon

Sift dry ingredients together into a large bowl. Add remaining ingredients and stir only enough to dampen the flour. The batter will not be smooth. Spoon batter into oiled muffin tins, fill about two-thirds full. Bake in 400° oven for 20 minutes. Makes 1 dozen.

MEADOW MUFFINS

2 cups sifted whole-wheat flour
2 T honey
2½ t baking powder
½ t salt
1 egg, well beaten
1 cup milk
¼ cup butter, melted and cooled slightly
1 cup ⅛-inch *alfalfa sprouts*

Sift flour, sugar, baking powder and salt together. Mix egg, honey, milk and butter. Add alfalfa sprouts to milk mixture, then pour into the dry ingredients. Mix only until flour is moistened. Spoon into well-greased muffin tins, filling the cups about two-thirds full. Bake in 400° oven for 25 minutes. Makes 1 dozen muffins.

RYE CRISPIES

2 cups *rye sprouts*
2 T butter
2 egg yolks
1 cup unbleached white flour
½ t salt

Grind sprouts, using fine blade, and mix with butter, egg yolks and salt. Stir in 1 cup of flour or enough to make a stiff dough. Knead until smooth and elastic. Cover and let stand on a floured board for 15 minutes. Roll out dough until very thin. Cut in rectangles, diamonds or squares and place on oiled cookie sheet. Bake in 400° oven for 10 minutes or until lightly browned. Makes about 4 dozen 1-inch by 2-inch crackers.

Variation: Before baking, sprinkle top of crackers with sesame or caraway seeds.

BREAD STICKS

1 T dry yeast
¾ cup warm water
1 t salt
1 T honey
1 cup *rye* or *wheat sprouts,* ground
2 cups wheat flour
¼ cup margarine
1 egg
1 T water
sesame, poppy or chia seeds

Dissolve yeast in a bowl of warm water. Add honey, sprouts, 1 cup flour and margarine. Beat until smooth; then mix in rest of flour. Knead on floured board until smooth, about 8 minutes. Place in a large greased bowl and cover with wax paper, then a clean towel. Let rise in a warm place (80° to 85°) for 1 hour or until double in bulk. Punch down and cut dough into 28 pieces; roll each into a stick 8 inches long. Place on a greased cookie sheet 1 inch apart. Beat egg with 1 tablespoon water; brush sticks with egg mixture and sprinkle with seeds. Bake 18 minutes or until golden brown in preheated 375° oven. Makes 28 sticks.

SPROUTED WHEAT BREAD

2 cakes yeast (2 T dry yeast)
2½ cups milk
¼ cup honey
3 T oil
1 T salt
5-6 cups whole-wheat flour
2 cups *wheat sprouts,* ground

Scald milk, then cool to lukewarm. Soften yeast in the warm milk. Add honey, oil and salt; mix well. Gradually add three cups of flour to yeast mixture and beat until elastic. Cover dough and let rise until double in bulk. Stir down and add sprouts and remaining flour. Knead dough until smooth and elastic, about 8 to 10 minutes. Put in oiled bowl, turning dough over to coat with oil. Let rise until double in bulk. Punch down and divide into loaves. Let rise in oil loaf pans until volume has doubled. Bake in preheated 375° oven for 25 minutes, or until loaves sound hollow when tapped with fingers. Remove from pans and cool on a wire rack. Makes 2 loaves.

DESSERTS

NATURE'S CANDY

¼ lb. dates
½ lb. dried figs
½ cup chopped walnuts
½ cup raisins
½ lb. dried apricots
1 cup *sprouted sunflower seeds*
1 T grated orange rind
⅔ cup shredded, unsweetened coconut

Grind all ingredients except rind and coconut. Mix well. Press into a buttered dish and cut into squares. Combine rind and coconut. Roll squares in the coconut mixture until well coated. Store in regrigerator. Makes about 2 pounds.

STUFFED PRUNES

1 lb. dried prunes
½ cup water
4 oz. cream cheese
1 cup *sunflower seed sprouts,* chopped
2 T orange juice

Cook prunes in water until tender. Cool. Whip orange juice and cream cheese together until smooth. Add sprouts and mix well. Cut prunes open on one side and remove pit. Fill prune cavities with cream cheese mixture. Chill before serving. Makes 4 to 6 servings.

DATE DROPS

¾ cup honey
½ cup margarine
1 egg
2 cups scotch oatmeal
1 cup flour
½ t soda
1 cup unsweetened coconut
1 cup chopped dates
2 cups *sunflower seed sprouts*
1 t vanilla

Cream honey and margarine. Add egg and vanilla; beat until smooth. Sift flour and soda together and add to honey mixture. Add remaining ingredients and mix well. Drop from a spoon onto a greased cookie sheet. Bake in a 375° oven for 10 minutes or until lightly browned. Makes 4 dozen.

ALFALFA COOKIES

¾ cup honey
½ cup tahini (a sesame seed paste or butter)
1 t vanilla
1 cup whole-wheat pastry flour
¼ t soda
½ t baking powder
1½ cups *alfalfa sprouts* (⅛″ long)
2 cups rolled oats, wheat or rye

Cream honey, tahini, and vanilla. Sift together flour, baking powder and soda. Add to honey mixture. Add remaining ingredients and mix well. Drop by spoonfuls onto a greased baking sheet. Bake in 350° oven until lightly browned, about 10 minutes. Makes 3 dozen.

CAROB BROWNIES

½ cup butter or margarine
⅔ cup honey
2 eggs, lightly beaten
1 t vanilla
½ cup carob powder
⅔ cup whole-wheat pastry flour
1 t baking powder
½ t salt
1 cup chopped walnuts
1 cup *alfalfa sprouts* (⅛" long)

Cream butter and honey. Add eggs, vanilla and sprouts. Sift together flour, carob, baking powder and salt. Add dry ingredients to egg and honey mixture. Mix well and fold in nuts. Spread batter in a 9 x 9 inch pan, which has been lined with wax paper. Bake in 350° oven for 30 minutes. Cut brownies while they are still warm. Serve plain or frost with carob frosting.

CAROB FROSTING

4 T evaporated milk
½ cup carob
4 T honey
4 T soft butter
1 t vanilla
½ cup chopped walnuts

Mix butter and carob. Blend in honey. When smooth, add milk and vanilla. Beat until creamy, then spread evenly over brownies and sprinkle with nuts. Frosting is excellent on cakes.

HONEY-NUT BALLS

½ cup sesame seeds
½ cup *sprouted sunflower seeds*
½ cup carob powder
½ cup peanut butter
½ cup honey

Mix all ingredients except sesame seeds. Rub a little butter on your hands and shape the candy into small balls. Roll candy balls into sesame seeds until coated. Chill until firm. Makes 24 balls.

BEVERAGES

RAW VEGETABLE DRINK

3 cups tomato juice
2 tomatoes, chopped
1 slice green pepper, chopped
½ cucumber, chopped
1 stalk celery, chopped
1 green onion, chopped
1 cup *alfalfa sprouts*

Liquify all ingredients in a blender.
Makes 5 cups. Serve as a beverage or
a soup.

SPROUT MILK

½ cup *sunflower seed sprouts*
¾ cup almonds or *almond sprouts*
2 cups cold water
2 T honey
salt

If unsprouted almonds are used,
soak them in water for 15 minutes
before blending. Put all ingredients
in a blender and liquify. Serve very
cold. Makes 2 servings.

AVOCADO DRINK

½ avocado
1 T lemon juice
1½ cups tomato juice
dash Tabasco
1 cup *alfalfa sprouts*

Put all ingredients in a blender and mix for 30 seconds. Makes about 2 cups. This drink is a meal in itself!

CHIA MARIA

2 cups tomato juice
2 T lemon juice
1 hot green chili, chopped (optional)
½ cup *chia sprouts*
dash Tabasco
salt
dash Worcestershire sauce,
  (optional)
Mix all ingredients in a blender for 30 seconds. For a summer cooler, serve over ice and garnish with a sprig of parsley. Makes 2 large glasses.

EAST-WEST WHIRL

For this refreshing beverage, use chia sprouts when *root* is only ⅛ inch long.

1 cup water
¾ cup plain yogurt
⅛ t dill weed
¼ cup *chia sprouts*
salt
pepper
4 ice cubes, cracked
2 sprigs of mint

Put all ingredients, except mint, in a blender and mix at high speed for 30 seconds. Serve in tall glasses. Garnish with a sprig of mint. Serves 2.

PINEAPPLE JUICE DRINK

½ cup *alfalfa sprouts*
1 cup unsweetened pineapple juice,
    chilled
1 T honey
½ ripe banana, cut up

Put all ingredients in a blender and
whirl at high speed for 10 seconds.
Makes 1 large serving.

DATE SHAKE

1 banana
1 cup milk
½ cup *wheat sprouts*
2 T wheat germ
1 T honey
4 pitted dates, chopped

Blend all ingredients for 1 minute.
Makes 1 serving.

POPEYE

¼ cup parsley juice
¼ cup carrot juice
¼ cup celery juice
¼ cup watercress, chopped
¼ cup spinach, chopped
1 cup *alfalfa sprouts*

Put all ingredients in a blender and
blend for 30 seconds. Serves 1.

WEIGHTS & MEASURES

dash or pinch . . . . Less than 1/8 teaspoon
3 teaspoons . . . . 1 tablespoon
2 tablespoons . . . . 1/8 cup
4 tablespoons . . . . 1/4 cup
5 tablespoons
+1 teaspoon . . . . 1/3 cup
8 tablespoons . . . . 1/2 cup
10 tablespoons
+2 teaspoons . . . . 2/3 cup
12 tablespoons . . . . 3/4 cup
16 tablespoons . . . . 1 cup
1 cup . . . . 8 fluid ounces
2 cups . . . . 1 pint (16 fluid ounces)
2 pints . . . . 1 quart (32 fluid ounces)
1 quart . . . . 4 cups
4 quarts . . . . 1 gallon
16 ounces (dry measure) . . . . 1 pound

Approximate Net Weight or Fluid Measure	Approximate Equivalent in Measuring Cupfuls
8 oz.	1 cup
10½ to 12 oz.	1¼ cups
12 oz.	1½ cups
14 to 16 oz.	1¾ cups
16 to 17 oz.	2 cups
1 lb. 4 oz. or 1 pt. 2 fl. oz.	2½ cups
1 lb. 13 oz.	3½ cups

INDEX

117